TEN-FINGER PRAYERS

THE AMAZINGLY TRUE STORY OF HOW AN ORPHAN BECAME AN OVERCOMER

AGNES ROBERTSON

Ten-Finger Prayers: The Amazingly True Story of How an Orphan Became an Overcomer

Forge

ISBN 978-8-9854126-5-9 (paperback)

ISBN 978-8-9854126-6-6 (e-book)

Published by Forge: Kingdom Building Ministries, 14485 East Evans Avenue, Denver, Colorado 80014

Written by Agnes Robertson.

Cover Design by: Katherine Parker Designs.

Visit us online at www.forgeforward.org

CONTENTS

CHAPTERS & STORIES

PREFACE

For most of my life I never told anyone the truth about my childhood.

It was a nightmare too painful to recall, and a story so filled with sorrow, I could only hate what few memories I allowed myself to recall of those awful days.

I had come to believe if people ever knew the real me, they would not like me. After all I had been nothing more than a number in a heartless system that treated children more like property than people. Overwhelmed by years of shame and embarrassment, my insecurities seemed insurmountable. How would I ever emerge from the shadows of my painful past and allow people to know and see the real me?

No more hesitation or delay. I believe the time has come to tell my story as it happened to me. I want to share with others the true account of my endless hard days and agonizing nights that left a little girl believing survival was her one and only goal in life.

That's an important story to tell. But I also want to tell another story —a better story, where the subject line doesn't begin with me but with the One who is the Author and Finisher of every good and grace-filled, well-ending story.

God did in my life what God alone could do. He changed my heart, my way of thinking, and the way I saw my life and this world. He performed miracle after miracle in my life—some seen by others, others only known by God and me. Some that took place quickly, others formed and fashioned over many years and siftings. I have come to the realization that life's most precious possession is not head-filled knowledge, hands filled with money, or social media pages filled with fame. No, life's most precious possession is a heart filled and overflowing with God's love. That's a story worth telling... and so I'm going tell it!

That is why I am reaching out to those whose hearts are broken as mine once was by neglect, abuse, and the absence of love in any form. I do so with the authentic love and care of Jesus who has changed my life so dramatically. I want you to know you were meant for more than just survival. Yes, God can rescue you from dark pits and desperate situations. And He will! God will also fill you with His Spirit, give you unspeakable joy, and use your *entire* story—the good, the bad, and the messy—to share His love and good news with others.

 For I know the plans I have for you, declares the Lord, plans for welfare and not for evil, to give you a future and a hope. — Jeremiah 29:11

Now in the sunsetting years of my life, there's a third reason I'm sharing my story. With God's grace, I pray my beloved children, grandchildren, and great grandchildren will remember the story of their grandmother and learn how Jesus can intervene in one's life in miraculous fashion. I want them to remember just as Jesus proved faithful to me in my darkest hours, He will prove faithful to them through all their life's sorrows and storms. And just as important, Jesus will help them live their lives to the fullest joy and potential as they seek Him, trust Him, and love Him more than anything else.

Finally, I want my family and all who read this to know that with Jesus, life is never a straight line. How we finish can become so different, so much better, than how we began. God's amazing grace, my life story, and the prayers connecting anyone and everyone to God's heart all testify to that truth.

INTRODUCTION

I believe in the power of prayer. I believe—not because prayer is magical, like rubbing a genie's bottle—but because I've witnessed firsthand what God does when people pray.

 Imagine your hands raised toward the heavens, your fingers slightly spread, your heart full. Your circumstance seems unsolvable, your words to God sincere. You've exhausted every resource. You have nowhere else to turn. Your mouth utters what your spirit longs for, "I can do all things through Christ who strengthens me." You repeat your prayer, stopping to emphasize each word: "I - can - do - all - things - through - Christ - who - strengthens - me." Your mind's eye falls on the words "can" and "all" and "Christ" and "strengthen" as God's Spirit encourages and empowers you. You begin to believe that God *will* make a way. He's got this. He has you. And perhaps most importantly, you aren't alone... God is *with* you.

That has been my life—not just praying the Apostle Paul's "Ten-Finger Prayer" from Philippians 4:13—but many prayers like it of various word counts and forms that have connected my heart to God's. Prayers prayed with hands raised (sometimes literally, other times symbolically) and with a most sincere heart. Prayers of desperation. Prayers of provision. Prayers for courage and faith. Prayers for decisions, healing, hope, and joy. Prayers for God's life-giving work in others. Prayers of worship and praise. Prayers for God to be glorified in all things.

For many years, prayer was *all* I had. In my younger days, God was my only hope in delivering me from life circumstance and heartache I wish for no one. In time, prayer became *everything* I had. Prayer became a lifestyle and moment by moment opportunity to know God and join Him in the good, gracious, and glorious things He was up to—in the world, in my neighborhood, in my family, and in my life.

Yes, I believe in the power of prayer. I also believe God answers prayer. Every prayer, every time. Perhaps not always in the way, delivery method, and timing I thought He might; but always answering, always—in beautiful, wonderful, life-giving, and trusted ways only God can know and design.

This book is a testament, a personal witness, to God's enduring faithfulness in hearing and answering prayer. Prayers prayed by discarded children, struggling parents, lost travelers, lonely wanderers, weary journeyers, and aging adults. Prayers by those deeply in love with God, Kingdom adventures, joy-filled laborers, knee-bent prayer warriors, and hands-raised worshipers. Prayers by those facing storms and difficult seasons as well as those enjoying life and ministry sweet spots... and all the people, prayers, places, and circumstances in-between.

If you find yourself in any of these prayers, maybe the chapters that follow will encourage and strengthen you. I originally wrote this memoir for my children, grandchildren, and the generations that follow. I wanted to let them know how good God is and how full and joy-filled life has been in knowing and following Jesus in all of life's ups and downs.

If you aren't related to me, please don't quit reading! There's something important I want you to know. I consider *you* my family too! I hope you'll pull up a seat and join in the telling of our faithful God who continues to answer prayer, make all things new, and make seemingly impossible things—possible!

DARK DESOLATE DAYS

DRINKING, DEFEATED, DAMAGED, DISCARDED

Supper was finished and the dishes were being washed by my mother who stood dutifully scrubbing and rinsing each one.

My little brother, Howard, the newest baby in the family, was watching us from his perch on the highchair. The other six children, including myself, were sitting on the floor stacking wooden blocks, drawing stick-figure people on paper, and arm wrestling with each other. It was a typical night in a midwestern home in the early days of the Great Depression. But, in so many other ways, my home life would prove to be anything but typical.

Suddenly, Father stomped into the room. Without warning he grabbed one of my older brothers by the arm and then yanked me up from the floor with his other free hand. He dragged the two of us toward the back door.

"Mom, where is Daddy taking them?" asked Ruby, my older sister.

"Dad's drunk again!" Mom cried out. "Hurry, everyone, run to your rooms!"

Dad nearly kicked open the back door as he walked out into the back alley hauling two terrified children in tow.

Shouting to no one in particular, his mad eyes glancing this way and then that way, he yelled at the top of his voice, "Kids for sale! Hardworking kids for sale!"

If the neighbors did hear his intoxicated rant, they pretended not to. No one took him up on his attempt to traffic his children for more liquor.

Dad was desperate for more drinking money and we were his only available collateral. No one came out to confront him directly, but a concerned neighbor immediately called the Social Welfare Office to report what they had just heard. Social Welfare had visited our home on several occasions before, and it usually ended with a warning followed by a shrug of indifference by my father once he closed the door.

However, this visit would end differently. This time all seven children would be taken from our home and parents—forever.

Little did I realize the day I was escorted down our driveway by state welfare employees that it would be the last day I would ever spend in our home with my family of origin. My world was about to change in a way I could never have imagined nor envisioned, even in my worst nightmares.

The day we left for good, my mother's face was empty and her emotions locked away somewhere beyond her reach. She went through the motions of bundling us up and then sent us out into the cold winter weather. What that must have done to her heart is beyond my knowing. How does the maternal heart of a mother continue beating (or even survive) when all seven of her children are suddenly taken from her in one day? My father's drinking and violent behavior must have so destroyed what was left of her personhood that she simply gave up. After that day, she never attempted to try to find us again.

I learned later from one of my siblings that this sad day when we were torn forever from one another had been a slow train coming. What started out as my mother simply trying to cope with her husband's addiction eventually became an unbearable ordeal that pushed her to the limits of her endurance and sanity—and then beyond.

With Social Services now involved, it became impossible to keep our family unit intact any longer. My father's bondage to alcohol eventually cost him everything in his life worth having. Mom went on to divorce my dad, start a new life for herself, and inexplicably leave her seven children in the rearview mirror to fend for themselves. Those who view alcohol as just another harmless beverage need to remember my father started out believing that as well.

My mother, Violet, had been warned not to marry my father (her third husband), but she married him anyway. The fact her two prior marriages had ended in divorce suggests she was raised with a damaged heart. Perhaps she felt unworthy of men who would treat her with love and respect. Not only was my father an alcoholic, but his father and mother died as alcoholics. Parents who are alcoholics cannot love their children and their addiction at the same time. One will always win out. In my father's case, his parents chose the bottle over their son. This is only an explanation, not an excuse for his detached and merciless behavior. But as someone once rightly said, "Pain rarely begins with us; it usually has parents and grandparents."

GOOD WILL FARM

Now officially a ward of the state of Michigan, my new home was the Good Will Farm, an orphanage cradled in the tall pine trees of the Upper Peninsula. It was located near Michigan Technological University and housed about 60 children at the time.

The Good Will Farm began in 1899 in the area known as Copper Country. Its purpose was to provide a safe home and school for orphaned children from the Upper Peninsula. The Good Will Farm was also aptly called *The Poor Farm*. Poor indeed, it was. Conditions were so stark, barren, and destitute that it was worthy of a Charles Dickens' novel.

"I carried you into the orphanage without any shoes on. You weren't even two years old at the time. It was winter and I didn't want you to get your feet cold and wet," said one of my older brothers decades later.

While we were well fed and kept warm at the Good Will Farm, that is where the "good will" seemed to end. Instead, we were forced to grow up with multitudes of other children without the love or security of their parents. While there was food on the table, there was little love or nurture in the room.

Soon every aspect of my life revolved around the Good Will Farm. Our school room, with its tattered desks and harsh teachers, were there at The Farm. Our doctor made house calls to examine us—not at his office—but at The Farm. Needed deliveries of food and other supplies arrived at the end of the long, winding driveway in front of The Farm. Life at The Farm was all I had or knew. We rarely went offsite. My world had suddenly gotten very small.

THE INFIRMARY

As many kids do, I came down with a bad case of measles. That was cause to send me across the dirt road to a dilapidated building called *The Infirmary*. The Infirmary was never a place one wanted to visit. It was always in our best interest to stay well, or if sick, pretend we were doing just fine. A case of the flu, strep throat, or measles easily landed us in the infirmary with a prolonged quarantine. With so many children on site, the last thing the orphanage wanted was an outbreak. So, they often took extreme preventative measures. Like the time I contracted the mumps. They isolated me in the ramshackle infirmary for three miserable weeks. I remember I was often unattended during that stay— left alone for long stretches without a nurse or adult to care for me.

I remember whispering one night to a fellow orphan recuperating in a nearby bed, "It's pitch dark in here, and I'm scared. The only toilet is in the basement, and the only light is a 'pole light' halfway down the steps. It's so eerie and spooky. I'm afraid to go down there by myself!"

"Go ahead, Agnes," came the voice from the dark, "cry really loud! The noise hides the sound of rats running across the floors."

Eventually, my fever broke, my swollen cheeks subsided, and I was released back to the dormitory.

LEMONADE FROM EARLY-LIFE LEMONS

Sadly, the days of loneliness and deprivation melted into months, and the months agonizingly turned to years. At the time, I had no idea what school grade I was in nor even what age I was. The orphanage didn't allow birthday parties, and the school never provided grades or guidance. The only feedback we ever received from teachers was when our answers were wrong. The school mandated the boys and girls lead separate lives. Such decisions only furthered the isolation we all felt.

It's no surprise that toys didn't exist to play with at the orphanage. I suppose, in one way, it increased our imagination and creativity. Occasionally, we managed to sneak in some fun apart from the gaze of our sober-faced state guardians.

Memories of a shiny, steel fire escape outside our dormitory still make my heart pound. Tip-toeing up the final set of stairs inside the fire escape, my heart would race as if it were leaving my body. I knew it was about to be my turn to "slide round 'n round all the way to the ground." I also learned the secret of sitting on a plastic Wonder Bread wrapper to zip down the circular steel slide at lightning speed!

The fun of sliding down the fire escape often came with the risk of getting caught. Once I ascended the stairs, I had to decide if I would quietly stay put or chance getting caught if I made my way down. It was all great fun… until the time one of the workers caught me. They made me go to bed without supper. But honestly, supper or not, the thrills were worth it! I love to this day how children can always find a way to have fun, even without toys.

PAIN AND DISTRUST ARE NO ACCIDENT

We shared a few "pets" among us. There were chickens to provide eggs, cats to chase the many rats, and bunnies for meat. The Farm's dog, an animal most would associate as a good companion for children, was tied on a long iron chain and served as a watchdog. Even "man's best friend" wasn't very children-friendly at The Farm.

I learned my lesson about the dog the hard way. Once, I innocently tried to pet the dog while he was sleeping. I must have startled him. He opened his eyes and lunged at my head, his teeth fully engaged. 85 years later, my forehead dons a big-scar reminder of the mistake I made that day.

Another event happened to me that may not have been so much an accident as an incident. I was standing beneath a tree one summer's day, when a boy yelled down to me from up in the branches, "Hey Agnes, can you get a pitchfork and hand it up to me?" he shouted.

I couldn't see who it was through the branches, but I wanted to help. "Sure thing," I replied.

Just as I handed the pitchfork up to him, he dropped it. It hit me right on the top of my head! The pitch fork made three, large bloody holes in my head. The orphanage workers shaved my head, stitched me up (though none of them had medical experience), and offered me no pain killers.

Yes, I survived those days. But with each cruel event and "accident" I endured, my trust in others withered. I began believing that the only one I could really ever trust was going to be myself.

OVERCAST DAYS TURN DARK: THE CATHOLIC ORPHANAGE

Despite all the daily hardships we lived with at The Farm, little did we know our darkest days were still ahead of us. It all began one day when I overheard the social worker and the orphanage director discussing what they called the "Catholic" family.

"Did you know the family of the seven children who came to live here two years ago was Catholic?" remarked the social worker to her supervisor.

"If that's the case," replied the orphanage director, "then the Catholics should take care of them."

Before we knew it, the seven "Catholic" kids with same last name were crammed into the back of the orphanage director's old, smelly car —I among them. Some workers made a feeble attempt to collect all our coats and shoes, and off we went to a place we did not know. I remember the sky as drab and dreary that day, the sun refusing to shine. The weather proved to be a sign of things to come.

The callousness of the director still breaks my heart today. "Happy and relieved" were the words he flippantly chose as he addressed the seven of us bewildered and frightened children in the back seat of his car. "We're happy and relieved," he said. "With you all gone, we now have seven less mouths to feed."

The car finally came to a stop just outside a huge stone edifice that looked like a hospital. We had arrived at the Holy Family Orphanage, a Catholic orphanage in Marquette, Michigan that housed over 200 children at a time. The orphanage was six stories high and had two separate basements. Fourteen nuns maintained order and managed the entire orphanage. Church, school, and housing were all on site.

NIGHTMARES MEANT FOR NO ONE

Little did we know it, but we were stepping into a nightmare far worse than the one we had endured at The Good Will Farm. Life immediately got worse. Nuns strutted about with whipping straps barely concealed beneath their black gowns in order to intimidate the children. They oversaw every move we made. The slightest misstep or misbehavior by any of us orphans and the straps came out. We constantly lived in fear. How adults charged with the care of vulnerable and defenseless children could resort to corporal punishment of the worst kind remains a mystery to me to this day.

Though I have found it in my heart to forgive my childhood tormentors, it is clear, behavior that now would land you in prison for physically abusing a child, was not only accepted but encouraged among the staff. Worse yet, the cruelty inflicted on us was done in the name of religion and somehow seen as virtuous. It was as if our Lord Jesus had never said that it would be better to have a millstone tied around your neck and tossed into the deepest ocean rather than inflict a deep wrong on a child (Luke 17:2).

I realize that my experience should not be used to typify or stereotype all individuals belonging to any religious order or tradition.

Yet, I must share the truth as it happened to me or I would be less than honest. If my experience can help insure nothing of this sort ever happens again, regardless of the religious affiliation involved, then retelling my experience as it happened will have served its intended purpose.

UNDIGNIFIED, UNSEEN, UNLOVED

Once I was settled into the new orphanage, I quickly realized there was no love to be found in this new place.

Something like animosity, bordering on hatred, seemed to flow through the veins of the nuns who daily were tasked with supervising all 200 children. As the days unfolded, I sadly realized I would be regarded as someone without personal value, unworthy of simple kindnesses, and undeserving of basic dignity. If any joy in life was going to be found, I was convinced that it would never be here.

Holy Family was a much bigger facility than The Farm. Still, the sanitary conditions were much worse, particularly in the kitchen and dining hall. Lunch was usually a little piece of meat and vegetables. The same meat and vegetables were served at supper as soup. Breakfast was always a bowl of oatmeal or Cream of Wheat.

"Have you seen the huge cockroaches climbing into the Cream of Wheat canister by the pot belly stove?" I whispered quietly to the girl next to me, "that's what the brown lumps in our cereal bowls are!" It was true too. And, as gross as the cockroaches were, I sometimes ate part of them.

After I told my table-mate about the "added protein," we both made a disgusted face. Unfortunately, we both understood there was no one to complain to and nothing we could do about it.

"Hey, I've got an idea," she said. "Let's use our spoons as slingshots and fling food at the smaller kids."

Regrettably, we found sport in terrorizing younger children with our pranks.

RAGAMUFFINS AND ROCKS

At Holy Family Orphanage we were less than four blocks from the largest and deepest of the Great Lakes, majestic Lake Superior. Yet, we never knew we were so close to such a remarkable jewel of nature. We were trapped like inmates in a high security prison, only allowed to leave the property once a year.

We had one annual outing a year. The local Marquette Lions Club sponsored us to walk to a movie theater in town. People in the community would gawk and stare at the ragged line of ragamuffins marching down the sidewalk. To get to the theater we would have to run a gauntlet of cruel teasing and heartless name calling by other children our age.

"Poor, ugly freaks! Why don't you join the circus?" called out one boy. His insult continued, "Oh no, too bad! Is it true they said they won't have you?"

"I would spit on you, but I don't want to waste my spit," jabbed another.

"They are animals, not people," laughed another.

"Dirty rocks to hit 'No Socks'!" yelled a group of boys as they threw handfuls of stones our way.

They did not need to go to the bother of reminding me I was inferior to the children who lived in town. I knew they had a home with their own belongings.

Truthfully, the insults and jeers didn't matter all that much to us. Most of us had heard it all before. All we cared about was enjoying the sights and sounds of a motion picture in a theater we had all to ourselves. We were determined to make the most of this one, brief opportunity to enjoy a little freedom provided but one time a year.

WITHOUT LOVE, WE LEARN TO HATE

Unfortunately, the indignities we endured proved much worse inside rather than outside of the orphanage. Each week, the girls were lined up and issued one dress for the week. The dress might be the same one our "worst enemy" wore the week before. The nuns didn't seem to care about how we felt about any of that. They treated us like we didn't deserve even the one garment a week we received.

As a young girl—utterly disconnected from any type of normal home life, or the love, care, or sense of personal identity healthy children need to thrive—my emotional growth became stunted. I learned that if I didn't hide my emotions, negative consequences followed. I often thought it would have been better if I were invisible to everyone around me. Worst of all, I learned to hate—hate everyone and everything around me. That is what can happen to a heart consistently deprived of love.

"All of you will be given chores hard enough to make you sweat," declared a nun. Staring menacingly in my direction she continued, "For you Agnes, your chore is to scrub the five stories of winding staircases every day to my satisfaction. I will not tell you how to do the stairs. You'll have to figure it out for yourself."

A second nun chimed in. "And I will beat you if you don't get every step done to perfection every day!" she snarled.

After a period of daily stair-cleaning, I was assigned to work in the newborn nursery, a job I did for years. Without proper training or instruction, I was expected to do my job to perfection. As a young girl, I was bound to make mistakes. And, of course, I did. The nun would reprimand me for everything and anything done wrong. Inconsequential oversights, such as a small piece of soiled cloth on the floor from a sick baby, would get me in trouble.

Perhaps a coincidence, perhaps not—but every year exactly nine months after the Annual Priest Convention at our orphanage, an influx of newborns were delivered. I'll have to leave the math and results of all that to God.

BEATEN UP AND BEATEN DOWN

The kids in the Holy Family Orphanage ranged in age from infants to seventeen years old. Brutal beatings were a daily occurrence. I knew this because I could hear the agonizing screams through the walls. I also knew because I received my own share of whippings.

At times, my back was so sore and blood stained, I had trouble sitting upright in a chair. I tried my best to obey the rules and requests, but sometimes I was beaten anyway. To this day I still have unsightly scars on my back from the buggy-whip beatings routinely handed out.

My environment encouraged only continual fear and confusion.

"Agnes, get inside the drum of this old washing machine and stay there until I tell you to get out," a nun once instructed. "While you're in there, do not talk to any of the children or look in their direction. You are different. In fact, you are much worse than the rest. So, if the time in this washer doesn't teach you your lesson, we'll think of another punishment for you."

Hard labor beat us down. We were all forced to manually scrub the main floors on our hands and knees.

If I was hurting or sick, I was too young to know how to communicate to an adult that something was wrong. Even if I could articulate it, no adults who felt safe were available to tell.

I seldom took time to "play." That was a foreign concept to me. Toys didn't exist nor was time given for leisure activities. I didn't really know how to play. But something in children becomes aware we were made to play, sing, laugh, and use our imagination. So, I taught myself to make the shape of a mouse out of a cloth the size of a man's handkerchief. I could make it appear to move and have life. It was a little hand trick I would use to entertain lots of children in future years to come.

BLURRY GOD PICTURES

Life became even more confusing when loveless and ungodly acts were connected to God—all in the name of religion.

Early before breakfast each morning, we were awakened to attend Mass. Each evening at 7:00 p.m. we were assembled in a large room and then marched to evening Mass. Like soldiers in a prison camp, we followed a strict daily regimen. We got up at the same time each day and went to bed at 8 p.m. immediately following evening Mass. Sun or rain, day and night we followed the same routine. Such breaks in schedule to enjoy a snack, eat popcorn or ice cream, or do something to break the monotony never happened.

As for our education, the nuns (as you might guess by now) had strict rules. They demanded perfection and no nonsense. "Agnes, you are not left-handed, you're just lazy," said a nun. "No one is left-handed. Every time I catch you using your left hand to write, I will give you a snap with a ruler on your hands and back."

 ### TEN-FINGER PRAYER PAUSE: UNSPOKEN PRAYERS

Prayer was foreign to me in my younger days. In fact, before living at the orphanage, prayers were nonexistent in my family. And while at the orphanage, prayers became something I learned, recited, and repeated. Prayers could be lumped into the same category of memorizing a poem, a periodic table, or a multiplication table. They were uninteresting and ineffectual—probably because of the people who misrepresented God by teaching one way and treating us orphans another. I had no idea prayer was something personal, powerful, and that put me close to the heart and mind of God.

While I didn't know what prayer was or how to prayer in my younger days, surely the prayers of others carried me. Perhaps your prayers for others you neither know nor have ever met will carry them.

* * *

DEEP WOUNDS, DAMAGING MESSAGES AND DEEDS

"Agnes, you are unwanted and no good," said another nun.

Did I believe them? Of course I did. Why wouldn't I? There was literally no one to tell me I was wanted, important, or loved. As a result,

I learned to pull my heart deeper and deeper inside a shell that I constructed to protect myself. My threatening surroundings always kept me on high alert.

The rigid organization of the orphanage forced us to go through daily life like cars on a Detroit assembly line. Take something as simple as brushing teeth. Each morning, we brushed our teeth with any one of 150 tooth brushes spread out on a table. It was a first-come, first-serve kind of deal when it came to which tooth brush we used.

Bath time came once a week. We bathed in groups of ten. From youngest to oldest, each child was assigned a number from one to ten. The bath didn't have running water, only a drain. So, water was hauled in and used quite sparingly.

The first child, *number one*, was called up and supplied enough water to soap up. Once lathered, more water—just enough to rinse—was trickled over the child. Once *number one* was finished, *number two* was called forward to bathe. Increasingly, the higher the number, the dirtier and colder the water became. Unfortunately, I remember being on the colder, dirtier end of the bath line far too often.

Then there was Mass. We hurried off to the chapel for Mass. During Mass, all the girls were forced to wear a headscarf. And, if we happened to doze off, we were jabbed or slugged by a nun to keep us awake.

With no parental love or family units to turn to for emotional support, orphanage gangs formed just to survive. Filled with rage from the constant abuse, we sometimes would fight with each other like mad raccoons.

One day, girls from an opposing gang pulled off my scarf head covering. It left a bobby pin dangling from my hair in the back. During Mass someone noticed the hanging bobby pin and pointed at me. A nun immediately called me out and took me to a room I had never seen before. The room was empty with a single chair in the center. The nun pulled out a horse whip and methodically whipped me for several minutes. My back was so bloody and torn. Life-long scars on my back still remind of that day.

Things like holy communion also sent mixed messages to us as children. Communion bread was given to us at morning and evening

Mass. However, only the priest was allowed to drink the wine. The thought behind it was that the priest would consume enough wine to "cover" all the children. With a lot of children comes a lot of wine drinking! It became clear, even to us as young children, that far too much wine was being consumed. I didn't know what to think of God by the nuns and priests who represented Him.

GRACE UNDER FIRE, GOD'S GOODNESS REMAINS

Despite the continual abuse, I somehow remained creative, fun-loving, and adventurous in spirit. All the darkness of my surroundings had yet to extinguish the child-like light within me. I can only credit this to the extraordinary grace of my loving Heavenly Father. Like Joseph in the Old Testament—despite all my family sorrows, abandonments, beatings, and betrayals, I chose to believe God had a purpose for my life. That belief often kept me from returning evil for evil.

CHRISTMAS BELLS AND ORANGE-BALL BABIES

Christmas music brought excitement to the air and would become my favorite memory. The nuns allowed us to listen to the radio during the week of Christmas. What a highlight for me. My heart longed after the joy Christmas celebrated.

"Jingle Bells! Jingle Bells! Jingle all the way!" blasted the radio. "Silent night. Holy night. All is calm. All is bright." Secular or sacred, I didn't care—each song hinted at a deeper joy available someday, somewhere beyond the orphanage.

Once a year, the Marquette Rotary Club paid for a big truck full of Florida oranges to be delivered to the orphanage. Each orphan received one of these highly coveted "orange balls."

I felt on top of the world when Christmas arrived and I was given my own orange! I loved my orange. In fact, I played with it like a favorite doll. I found slivers of wool and toilet paper and dressed it up like a baby. I took small streaks from the ink well and colored a head of black hair. I even slept with it! My orange was like my newborn baby doll in my bed.

One day I noticed a white spot on the orange. I knew it was dying. I never viewed the orange as a food item. Instead, it was my very own prized possession, my special companion. I looked forward to my new orange every year.

Even now, oranges at Christmas represent a wonderful time of year for me. It's a time when music breaks through the pain and silence. The smell of an orange today still reminds me that Jesus came to us as a sweet little baby—bringing hope, comfort, and cheer with His arrival.

AS FOREIGN AS SPACESHIPS AND ALIENS

It is hard to describe how orphans view themselves. I had no sense of belonging, no knowledge of where I was from, who I was, or who my people were. Titles such as "relative, aunt, uncle, mom, or dad" meant nothing to me. People were just people. How they intersected and related just didn't register. For instance, I loved watching the altar boys during Mass. They seemed fun and interesting, and coincidentally, some of them shared my last name. Still, I never put it together they were actually my flesh-and-blood brothers! Being orphaned had taken its toll. The concept of "brother" or "sister" was as foreign to me as spaceships and aliens (and would remain so for many years).

I was an orphan and learned what many orphans do: give up on ever having a family or place to belong.

At a young age, I had lost all hope of loving and being loved, of belonging to anyone or any kind of "family."

That was, until ...

2

DIVINE RESCUE

WHAT'S AN "AUNT AND UNCLE"?

"Agnes, your aunt and uncle are here to see you," a nun bellowed up the stairs in my direction.

Being called by name to come downstairs was always an anxiety-producing moment for any of us orphans. But this time the nun's voice seemed to lack the usual tone I was used to hearing when I was in trouble again for something.

"What's an aunt and uncle?" I yelled back down the stairs.

Believe it or not the meaning of those titles was as foreign to me as if I had been addressed in Portuguese or Mandarin Chinese. Normal family names, much less normal family relationships, did not exist in my world. So, I was genuinely perplexed by who these people were.

Seeing my feet appear at the top of the steps, the priest requested I come downstairs to meet my guests. He, like the nun, was a bit more cordial than I was used to.

AUNT ORTHA, UNCLE ERNEST, AND HOPE

"Agnes, please meet your mother's sister and her husband," said the nun respectfully. "This is your blood relative, Aunt Ortha, and her husband, Uncle Ernest. Please say, 'Hello.'"

You would have thought for the moment the orphanage had suddenly transformed into a charm school for young debutantes to learn good manners and proper etiquette.

"Hello, Aunt Ortha and Uncle Ernest," I said meekly, my eyes staring down at the floor out of discomfort and fear. Orphans learn quickly to never make eye contact with superiors—a lesson I had mastered for years.

"Since school is out, could Agnes come with us for the summer?" Aunt Ortha asked sweetly. "We will bring her back right away if she is not happy. I promise."

The nun appeared unsettled by the request and remained silent. The priest, however, spoke up. "Well, I don't see why not," his hands folded in his typical reverent posture. "I mean, summer classes aren't in session, and…" he hesitated, "it's one less mouth for us to feed!"

Polite laughter dotted the room. Perhaps I was the only one that realized he meant exactly what he said.

"Agnes, let's get you some clothes so you can go for a visit," said the nun. Her syrupy kindness continued to drip.

So out of character was everyone's behavior that I really didn't know what to make of all that was happening. "Thank you," I said quietly. I thought a simple and sweet response gave me the best chance of not having the invitation revoked by something I said.

"We come from the Lower Peninsula in Vassar, Michigan, not quite as far south as Detroit," Uncle Ernest interjected.

I, of course, had no earthly idea where Vassar, Michigan was located. I had spent my entire life in the Upper Peninsula. As far as I was concerned, every other place in the United States was just a colored map I would never get to visit. I had resigned to living out the rest of my days in this remote and lonely place.

Feeling a bit more certain his guests were serious about removing me from the orphanage, the priest shared more transparently about his core philosophy regarding a child's value:

"You can get a lot of work out of her," affirmed the priest. "Yes, indeed. Summer is a good time for her to visit so she can help you around the house and yard. She's a hard worker, I dare say."

My aunt and uncle glanced at each other with a mixture of confusion and concern that a man of the cloth would view a young girl in such a way. They had no idea how many more disheartening details of my ordeal would emerge over the next weeks, months, and years. They seem to take a que from me that words might only get in the way of taking me home. So, they said nothing and politely nodded instead.

The nun who offered to find some clothes for me re-entered the room holding a brown grocery bag. She presented her findings as if she had been searching through my wardrobe for just the perfect summer outfits. "Let's see," she said, "there are three dresses, two underpants, two pair of socks, and a good pair of shoes. This A&P bag has everything you need for your visit."

The nun smiled with the satisfaction of someone who sends the best of the Thanksgiving leftovers home with their guests after a sumptuous meal. She carefully handed the bag with the garments neatly folded inside to Aunt Ortha.

"We are most grateful. Thank you so much for your assistance," my aunt replied in polite fashion.

The nun smiled, bowed, and slowly backed out of the room.

THE SECOND MOST IMPORTANT DAY OF MY LIFE

I quickly walked out the door with the two strangers who had displayed more kindness to me in ten minutes than I had received from the orphanage in ten years. I dared not look back. Fear gripped my throat and restricted my breathing. I knew each step forward toward freedom might be thwarted by a last-second reversal by the whim of the priest or a nun.

Most orphans in our home learned to adjust expectations regarding happiness. The belief was basic: *good things happen for children born into regular families, but not for us.* We orphans were convinced that we were born to live out some kind of different reality, one removed from the daily joys of life. Simple joys like having breakfast with warm toast and butter, family around the dinner table, the security of being tucked snuggly into bed with a parent reading a fun story, or turning out the lights after a reassuring prayer—these things were for other kids, but not for us.

I was among those who came to believe they belonged in a different category than "normal" kids. Perhaps I had known too many disappointments, too many moments stolen from my childhood, too many dreams crushed at the last moment. All I knew was that good things didn't happen to me. They weren't allowed to, not according to my given place and station in life. That's why it was hard to believe this was actually happening.

But it was.

With one last stride and a giant leap, I jumped into the back seat of the car. The door thumped quickly behind me. The sweet smell of the cloth interior instantly caught my attention. My mind harkened back to the stench of the car that delivered me to Holy Family. This car smelled like flowers. That car smelled like death.

As good as all this was seeming, I dared not let myself feel hope of any kind. What if this was just a cruel hoax? What if the promise of freedom and family was yanked mercilessly from me at the last moment?

As my mind raced in many directions, the kind man they said was my uncle turned the key of the ignition. The engine of the 1930's automobile sounded like faraway thunder on a summer night. The car came to life. And so did my hope.

Looking back, I can say without hesitation—next to the day I prayed to receive Christ as my Savior—no single event has changed my life more than this day, the day someone unexpectedly called my name up a flight of stairs.

LIKE A CARRIAGE RIDE TO THE BALL

Not long into our ride, I began taking inventory of my surroundings. The cushioned cloth seats were the first clean ones I could remember sitting on. The door had a polished steel handle for cranking down the thick glass window. In front of me was a pocket carefully sewn into the back of the seat with a road map protruding from it. The visor was folded down in front of Aunt Ortha's face to deflect the mid-afternoon sun. The light washed over her face in a way that made her glow like an angel. As far as I was concerned, she was.

The car may have been older and used. It may not have fancied the gadgets today's cars have. But to me, this car was my royal chariot, and I was a princess on my way to Buckingham Palace.

Still, despite the kind people, pleasant surroundings, and hopeful dreams that transported me to a different world (if not a different universe), a quick inventory of my emotions brought me back to my orphaned reality. My external circumstances were changing rapidly, but my internal world remained sadly familiar.

COLD HEART, CORN, AND COBRAS

My heart felt cold, like I was carrying around a bitter and angry stone where the tender heart of an innocent and carefree child should reside. How could I feel otherwise? Over time, my heart had calcified and detached from all feelings. After too many years of rejection, cruelty, unanswered questions, isolation, disappointment, and violent abuse, I could not trust anyone—not even the two heaven-sent messengers in the front seat sent to rescue me.

Passing farm after farm and row after row of knee-high corn fields, the trip began to ease and my heart settle. I started to reflect on the last hour of my life at the orphanage. Admittedly, the nuns and the priest had been nice to me in front of my uncle and aunt. Why couldn't they have spoken nicely to me, even just once, when no one was looking? Why the apparent show for these outsiders? What was it they wanted these visitors to think about their treatment of me through all these years? That I was living in one big happy family?

The corn rows were straight. My mind, however, swerved back and forth from safety to confusion, from familiar to unknown, from hopeful to fearful. Perhaps most vexing was the hideous movie reel that kept looping in my mind. It was the scene where I am sitting in a chair and a nun pulls a cobra out from under her robe. The cobra, mouth wide open, is poised to strike. I knew this movie well—the cobra was a curled black horse whip, and I was its prey. I guess as fast as Uncle Ernest's car was, it couldn't outrun the physical and emotional pain inflicted all those years.

A fortunate bump in the highway jarred me back to reality. The task at hand was to adjust to a world ignorant of and unprepared to encounter. Whatever lay ahead, it could not possibly be worse than what lay behind. That much I knew.

A WHOLE NEW WORLD

I leaned my nose against the window and drank in the world I had now suddenly joined. With what seemed like lightning speed we shot past huge houses, barns, cars, and trucks. Prior to this, my only expedition into the outside world from the orphanage had been my yearly trip to the movie theater at Christmas time. Every sight and sound mesmerized me. The wonderful things that existed beyond the prison-like world I left were unfathomable.

It was an eight-hour ride from the northwestern section of the Upper Peninsula of Michigan to the southeastern part of the Lower Peninsula. I sat in wonder as the reality of my first day of freedom unfolded. Our first stop was a roadside park that featured outhouses and red picnic tables. We feasted on bologna sandwiches made with soft white bread, munched on red crisp apples, and sipped lukewarm water in blue Mason jars. This was my first taste of "heaven on earth." There was more to come in the days ahead—more than I could ever have imagined.

MANY THINGS BURIED IN PANSY'S CASKET

I rejoiced in my newfound freedom with each mile that passed. That said, my thoughts kept going back to the horrible room at Holy Family Orphanage where I had received my worst beating. I had been taken to that room just one month earlier to see my friend, Pansy, after she had gone missing for several days from the orphanage. Two nuns who knew I was Pansy's best friend brought me to the room without telling me why. As soon as I stepped through the door, I knew. To my utter horror, Pansy's body, motionless and lifeless, lay before me.

Were the nuns showing me Pansy to scare me? Was it some type of silent confession because they had committed some unspeakable crime? Was it some type of perverse act of mercy so I could say a final good-bye to dear Pansy? To this day, I don't know. No words were ever spoken. The two nuns remained stoic as they watched me sobbing deeply for my best friend.

I had endured many unanswered questions as an orphan, but this act of cruelty was far beyond anything I could even begin to comprehend. Why in the world would anyone hurt dear Pansy? She was one of the few rays of sunshine in that dark place. What did she do to deserve such an ignoble end? Was her crime having a sweet and gentle spirit that brought life and light to dark places?

After that traumatic event, I pushed every thought of Pansy in her casket to deep and unretrievable places in my heart. The emotional, Mack-truck impact was more than I could bear. I also feared that talking about Pansy's event publicly might cause me to suffer the same fate.

Who knows what might have happened to me had Aunt Ortha not showed up when she did? Yet, with each passing hour of our ride, instinctively I knew I was safe in the care of the two kind persons steering and navigating the "chariot of freedom" we were traveling in.

If only Pansy had been in the seat next to me.

KISSED BY GOODNESS, GRACE, AND GOATS

The afternoon melted into the red glow of a summer sunset. The sound of gravel crunching under the car tires alerted me we were close to our destination. Easing up the driveway, my uncle stopped the car, moved the gearshift to "Park," and turned off the ignition. We had arrived at my aunt and uncle's home in the Lower Peninsula town of Vassar, Michigan. Had I been Cinderella stepping from her gold-trimmed carriage to enter the castle of the Prince, I could not have been more enthralled by what I saw.

Ernest and Ortha lived on a small farm. The white farmhouse featured several rectangular windows, a steep second-story roofline, and a weathervane that spun in the wind. The notion that this would be the place I'd be staying was both magical and hard to comprehend.

Once inside, Aunt Ortha gave me a tour of their home. I was amazed at every corner turned, every discovery made. The tour's grand finale came as Aunt Ortha turned the doorknob to a breathtaking room and announced, "This is your room."

Inside stood a big iron bed with a beautiful handmade quilt that fell to the floor on three sides. My entire life I had been sleeping on a child-size cot. Not anymore. The oversized mattress was so wide that four of us orphans could have slept side by side and still had room! That evening, as my aunt and uncle tucked me into bed, Aunt Ortha leaned over and kissed me on the forehead. Uncle Ernest turned off the light, and they gently closed the door behind them. My heart was full. As the sounds of their steps faded down the hallway, I burst into tears. I couldn't contain the love and gratitude that filled my soul. No one had ever kissed me goodnight before—ever.

My tears expressed what my lips could not. I was loved. I was wanted. I was free of the dark walls of the orphanage. And, for the first time in my entire life, I had a room all to myself!

The next morning, after a delicious breakfast of eggs and cereal (with no insects in the Cream of Wheat!), I was informed I could go outside and lay on a special red blanket spread out *just for me*. So I did just that. I enjoyed the sweet aroma of flower bushes blooming on a summer's morning and stared at the sky. I imagined shapes and faces made of silky clouds that lazily drifted by. As one particularly beautiful cloud passed by, I thought for a moment I could see the face of Pansy, looking down on me and smiling.

My deep breaths and joyous imaginations were soon disrupted by my boy cousins who wanted to play a fun-loving prank on me. Unlike the cruel jokes played on one another at the orphanage, this prank was intended to surprise me and make me laugh. The boys let the family goat out of its pen. The goat quickly ran over to me, and began nuzzling me with its nose. I couldn't help but giggle. I had never been so close to a Billy goat in all my life. Unlike the snarl-toothed guard dog at the orphange, this creature was friendly and playful. I squealed with delight.

HORNETS, NAILS, AND LOTS OF LOVE

The goat, meaning no harm, became more friendly than I was comfortable with. So, I jumped up on an old tractor seat nearby. I pretended I was driving, but somehow aggravated a hornet's nest underneath the seat. They swarmed out of their nest like a fire truck responding to a four-alarm call. The hornets chased me all the way to the house.

When I reached the backdoor, I accidentally stepped on a board with a nail sticking up. The nail went straight through the bottom of my foot. Pain shot up my leg. The yellow and green socks I was wearing quickly turned red and purple from my oozing blood.

My aunt and uncle somehow worked the metal nail out of my foot. I tried to sleep that night, but by morning I was running a high temperature. Unlike past days when I would have been shuttled off to an empty infirmary across an old dirt road, my new guardians immediately loaded me into the car and raced down the road to see the town doctor.

My first 48 hours of freedom found plenty of trouble. But honestly, I did not care. The nail driven through my foot hurt drastically less by comparison than the nail driven through my heart over and over again at the orphanage. My new world was now a place where fun, love, laughter, and kindness were the order of the day. I felt like heaven came to greet me.

FLUFFY, MUFFY, MOLLIE, AND HOLLIE

I made many discoveries in those early days on the farm, one being how my Uncle Ernest enjoyed raising rabbits. One day, my aunt and uncle informed me we would be moving up the road into the church parsonage. *What's a parsonage?* I remember thinking. That quandary was quickly replaced by Aunt Ortha's next bit of news. "There is no place to raise rabbits at our new place," she said, "so we will just have to kill the rabbits and can use them for meat this coming winter."

Fighting back tears, I pleaded with Aunt Ortha, "Please, no! I can't bear to watch my babies die. Not Fluffy, Muffy, Mollie, Hollie, Dollie!" I said fighting back tears. I had named each and every one.

"Our fenced-in rabbits will die if we let them out in the wild," Aunt Ortha replied. She continued to explain, "They just aren't used to the woods and fields and can't fend for themselves. And truthfully, we badly need the food."

"I am so sorry, Agnes," Uncle Ernest said with compassion in his voice. A sorrow in his eyes told me that Uncle Ernest understood my pain. Sympathy for my hurts was not something I was used to. I nodded my head in sorrowful agreement. As a way of saying my last goodbyes, I went and played with the rabbits one more time.

MORE THAN CLOTHES IN THE A&P BAG

It took time to get adjusted to life beyond the orphanage. There were just so many differences! For one, I was so used to itching and scratching all the time. I just assumed itching was normal. Everyone itched all the time at the orphanage. My itching and scratching continued day and night on the farm. It wasn't long until my uncle, aunt, and all my cousins were itching too. After some deducing and diagnosis, we discovered I had brought more with me in my brown

A&P grocery bag than just clothing. I had also transported live bed bugs, lice, and fleas.

The home remedies in those days for the "itchings" were in some ways as bad as the affliction itself. To cure us all of these uninvited guests, my aunt and uncle poured kerosene on our heads and covered us with a towel (and reminded us to stay outside and away from any fire!). Oh, how the kerosene burned my skin! But, lo and behold, it did the trick. Not even white lice can withstand a bath of liquid petroleum. Every one of us ended up smelling like smoking lanterns on the porch at night. It was well worth being rid of our unwanted tag-alongs from the orphanage.

AUNT ORTHA AND THE UPRIGHT PIANO

Life at the church and parsonage was fun for me. One of my greatest joys was to watch my aunt play her heart out on an old, wooden upright piano at the church. Her posture straight and gaze focused on the sheet music, she would occasionally glance and smile at me as she played. I loved to sit in those dark-stained wooden pews and watch Aunt Ortha's hands glide across the piano keys as the sun gleamed through the windows like rays from heaven.

On Sundays, when Aunt Ortha played congregational hymns, the people sang with such gusto and joy. I resolved right then and there that someday I would play the piano just like her.

JUDGEMENT DAY WITH THE ORPHANAGE

As summer wore on, a nagging thought kept returning. *When the summer is over*, I wondered, *will I be sent back to the orphanage?*

Just the thought of even driving by the property, much less turning into the orphanage driveway, twisted my stomach in knots. My aunt and uncle must have sensed my concern. Without my asking, about one month after I arrived, Uncle Ernest wrote a letter to the priest at Holy Family Orphanage. He asked if it would be okay if they did not bring me back.

The priest wrote back, "Sure! You just need to go and talk to your local priest."

Uncle Ernest shot a letter back, "But we aren't Catholic!"

The priest replied with some worrisome news, "Then you will have to bring Agnes back, because the judge here in the Upper Peninsula is looking for her."

Uncle Ernest, rather than being discouraged, saw this as an opportunity to strike while the iron was hot. He put the letter down with the look of a man on a mission. The very next day he piled us all into the car and headed up north. He had decided he would talk to the judge in person once he got to the Upper Peninsula.

The mood inside the car was understandably quiet and somber. As the oak and maple trees of lower Michigan began to give way to the white birch trees and towering pines, the tension grew inside us all. Would this be the last time I would ride in this wonderful car with these wonderful people? Or would I finally be set free to enjoy the new life God had so unexpectedly gifted me?

Thankfully, the judge's ruling was favorable. Since no one from my family of origin or other couples were actively pursuing to adopt me, it was fine for my nearest of kin to keep me. Then he pointed his gavel at my uncle and solemnly warned him, "If they ever catch Agnes within ten miles of the orphanage, they can legally take her back there."

That was all Uncle Ernest needed to hear. He immediately piled us into the car and made a beeline south. He drove away from the reach of the orphanage as fast as the car could legally travel (and perhaps a little more than that). The orphanage and all its unending sorrows and torments was finally receding in the rearview mirror—this time for good.

VISITING VIOLET

As we started to drive home toward Vassar, Aunt Ortha said what had been on her heart for some time, "My hope and desire is to find my long-lost sister, Violet. Hopefully, she's somewhere in this area."

I had dozed off in the backseat of the car and was jostled awake when the purr of the engine became silent. Aunt Ortha looked at me and said with her sweet smile and soft eyes, "Agnes, we're going to visit a relative of ours who lives here."

Their hearts were no doubt trembling as we walked together up the narrow dirt sidewalk to Violet's place. "Violet" was the real name of my birth mother. I had no idea who she was at the time, but that's where we were—the house of my birth mother. I may not have known why we were there or who we were actually visiting, but I remember feeling the emotional weight of my aunt and uncle's spirits. I sensed that the person we were visiting must be important, a key "lady" in my past and/or future. Yet, no one told me why that was or what we were doing there. I'm sure now they were only trying to protect me given the unpredictable nature of the situation.

Ortha had not seen her sister in a long, long time. I could sense her nervousness. I thought I heard her uttering a prayer as she knocked on the door. We waited for what seemed an eternity for someone to appear.

When the door finally creaked open, we were met by a woman with gray hair and hollow eyes. She glanced at my aunt and uncle, and then she looked at me. A mixture of curiosity and sadness blanketed her deeply wrinkled face. Seeing her face to face gave no added insight. I had no idea who this frail-appearing, elderly person was.

"Won't you all come in?" she said quietly.

She led us down a narrow hallway to a humble kitchen that had a few chairs, a simple white tablecloth, and a few apples in a woven basket. The almost barren room had few if any pictures on the walls. I took note of her understated appearance. She wore a plain dress with an apron strapped on top.

I recall one other memory of this encounter. I remember noticing the absence of any kind of nun's uniform. Neither a robe or habit were anywhere to be found in this exceedingly small house in the middle of nowhere.

How a child can forget the face of their mother remains a mystery to me. It is against the natural order of things. Yet, most of my childhood had been against the natural order of things. Why my mother allowed me and all her children to be taken, and why she never visited the orphanage to see any of us, even just for an hour, is one of my life's great mysteries. It flies in the face of all I know of maternal instincts. Something must have happened in her heart that was so awful, so tragic, so unspeakable, that only our loving Father could explain such an unnatural detachment.

The atmosphere in the kitchen was heavy. My aunt glanced nervously at the floor. Too full to keep it all inside, she blurted out, "Violet, I am your sister, Ortha."

Ever since Violet had decided to marry a man her parents vehemently disapproved of and left home never to return, she had had no further contact with any of her siblings or parents. As far as Violet was concerned, she was dead to all of us.

I listened carefully as the two women spoke about many things, including their oldest sister, Catherine. There were so many puzzle pieces for my young mind to fit together and make sense of. Then came this disheartening news. "Your brother fell out of a tree," said Aunt Ortha, "He's dead."

Despite the in-person visit and all the dialogue that followed, this woman named "Violet" was still a stranger to me. She was just a person I had never met and would likely never meet again. I felt no familiarity toward her, and with that, no love. All the years of excruciating pain, abandonment, and broken-hearted living veiled the face of the one who carried me in her womb, gave birth to me, and nurtured me in my earliest years of life.

THE STRANGE LITTLE GIRL IN THE ROOM

For her part, Violet never spoke my name or acknowledged my presence in any personal or endearing way. Rather, she seemed to force herself to look away. Everyone at the table *knew* who I was and what had been done to seal my orphaned fate, but Violet seemed determined not to acknowledge the "little girl in the room."

As for me, I was too young to understand the meaning of the moment. Despite the fact so many years had passed and so much damage had been done, little of the painful truth was spoken that day. This woman, whoever she was, appeared to know nothing of the way I was torn from my home and sent to an emotionless, calloused place where love was never offered, felt, or exchanged.

Did my birthmother ever wonder how things had been for me since that terrible day? Why was there no shame on her face? No grief? No sorrow? It would have meant so much to me to hear a mother's grief even for a moment. I could have accepted, perhaps forgiven her, had she confessed she was just a desperate woman in dire circumstances doing best she could at the time.

But that day, there was only silence. Only distance. Only a vacant stare that made me believe I was just another stranger to her. Violet's feelings toward me were no different than if I were just another young girl she passed on a city street.

Perhaps, just perhaps, things had become so desperate and overwhelming in her life that she believed my siblings and I would receive better care as wards of the state. That any existence would be better for us than the nightmare of living with a violent alcoholic father. Perhaps, she believed it was severe mercy to send us away from an unpredictable, chaotic, and dangerous home.

As for Violet's "mother heart"? Perhaps it was so broken, so devastated, and so exhausted by decades of spousal abuse, she simply lost the will to go on. Perhaps my mother's heart for her children simply quit beating.

Often, I have pondered the unknown of my birthmother's life and choices. Since becoming a mother myself, I have made my peace by believing, "She must have done the best she could."

This is where my faith as a Christian has been such a comfort to me as I have passed through life's many adversities. I have come to believe sometimes the only option we have is to lay our unanswered questions before God's throne and think the best of others.

I will confess I remain mystified why any mother, especially mine, would abandon all seven of her children. Yet, I rest in the knowledge that one day our Lord Jesus will explain everything to us. And, when He does, we will agree all things ultimately worked together for our good and His glory.

As the hours passed at Violet's home the topic of overnight lodging came up. There were few hotels in rural areas in the 1940s. That was true for Iron County where Violet lived. As a result, she invited us to spend the night at her house, and my aunt and Uncle agreed.

THE GRAY-HAIRED LADY IN THE ROCKING CHAIR

That night, I was given a place on the couch to sleep. What happened next, I will never forget. For some reason, I woke up in the middle of the night. As my eyes began to adjust from having been asleep, I could see in the dim light of the room the gray-haired lady whose home we were visiting. She was sitting in a rocking chair across from me.

The gray-haired lady kept looking at me and crying. I had no idea why. It spooked me a little. So, I did the only thing I knew to do. I just turned away, pulled the blanket up over my head, and went back to sleep. How long she stayed beside my bed I will never know. Now, a lifetime later, I can only imagine how difficult that night must have been for her.

At dawn, we quickly got our things together to begin heading home. I was eager to leave and glad we didn't linger. The walk to the car was filled with wonderings about what our visit was really all about. Decades later, I was told how I met my birthmother that strange and fateful day. Sadly, that day was the last time I ever saw her.

SCHOOLHOUSE BELLS AND FIRE BRIGADES

When we arrived back home, my Aunt Ortha informed me I would be attending a one room schoolhouse in the fall. That news was sheer delight to my ears! I would be learning with students from first to eighth grades in this small, white building down the road from us.

Soon enough, the lazy days of summer ended and school began. Not long after the school year started, a fire broke out and was getting perilously close to engulfing the town in its fiery claws. The school alarm sounded, class was abruptly dismissed, and we were immediately sent out to help the volunteer fire department. Our job was to join a line of local townspeople who formed a long and winding water brigade. The smell of smoke was strong, and the heat in the wind continued to get hotter. In the end, however, our community effort was successful. Not a single building in town was destroyed.

FINNISH FRIENDS AND SAUNA HUTS

Michigan in those days was home to first and second-generation immigrant groups. Close to where we lived, families from Finland had settled. The Finnish people were kind to us and let us use their little outdoor sauna huts to take hot steam baths year-round, even in the winter. We would sit huddled inside as the steam hissed off the heated rocks filling the room with moist heat and fog with temperatures inside reaching well over 100 degrees.

The Finns had a custom of taking freshly cut birch branches and brushing themselves all over their skin to improve circulation. It was an exhilarating feeling of refreshment on one's skin, which is hard to describe.

When it got too hot inside and we couldn't take the heat any longer, we would burst out the door of the sauna yelling and screaming at the top of our lungs. With great delight, we'd plunge into the river. We would repeat this crazy Scandinavian ritual until we were all exhausted. It was such great fun!

TRIAL VISIT, NEW TRANSITIONS

Sometime later, a brother of Ernest's—Uncle Archie and his wife, Erma —arrived to visit us at the parsonage. They had never been able to have children of their own. After dinner, all the adults sat around the lace-draped kitchen table and talked over fruit pie and coffee.

It was then I overheard them discussing and deciding that I was to go and live with Aunt Erma and Uncle Archie for four weeks. *[I would not become aware for decades later that their visit coincided with my dear Aunt*

Ortha apparently having suffered a "nervous breakdown," something never spoken of and kept hushed for years.] As I listened to the serious back and forth at the table, it sounded like my month-long visit would be a trial to see how we all got along.

While I sensed they cared about me and were only seeking what was best, I can honestly say I loved being right where I was—with my mother's blood sister, Aunt Ortha, and my Uncle Ernest. Years later, I learned my Uncle Ernest wept repeatedly over my departure from their family and home.

While I knew my aunts and uncles sincerely loved me, I once again had to navigate the fact that I was being "given up." I would soon be placed in a new set of unfamiliar people and circumstances.

Fortunately, this time was different.

I had come to implicitly trust my Aunt Ortha and Uncle Ernest. I knew beyond a shadow of a doubt they would never do anything to harm me. I was their precious Agnes. They had been—and would always be—my rescuers from the orphanage. I knew no one could ever replace them in my heart.

I left with Aunt Erma and Uncle Archie for the month-long trial of living with them. They lived on a fruit farm in Beulah, Michigan, a lush farming area near the bigger city of Traverse City.

To grow up under the watchful care of Aunt Erma and Uncle Archie (who had no children of their own) would be, all things considered, the best place for me. With Aunt Ortha living in a fragile and depleted emotional state, I can understand how she and Uncle Ernest believed it was good for me to experience farm life in the great outdoors.

As usual, Aunt Ortha and Uncle Ernest were right.

3

BEULAH LAND

BEULAH LAND AND BICYCLES

Beulah, Michigan became my Beulah Land. Once I moved to Aunt Erma and Uncle Archie's fruit farm, I learned to pick cherries, apples, and strawberries. I received modest pay for my labor and saved the money to buy my first bicycle. When I arrived home from town with my brand-new, shiny and blue bicycle, all the neighbors came over to see it. Blue was not only my favorite color, but the bike was the fulfillment of a lifelong dream to own something of my own.

"Hey Agnes! Do you know how to ride a bike?" asked my cousin, Guy Rayle.

"Sure!" I said. "Of course, I know how to ride my bike. Why else would I have bought it?"

"I'm going to ride with you," said Guy. "It works best to get going at the top of the hill to start."

"I can ride a bike perfectly fine," I retorted.

Guy insisted. "I'll sit in back so I can give you a little push," he said.

We did as Guy described. I sat in front and Guy behind me to "give a little push." What followed was two screams and a crashing sound that split the afternoon quiet. Aunt Carrie came tearing out of the house to see Guy and me on the ground and the bike tipped over with wheels spinning in the air. Thankfully, the only thing wounded that day was my pride. I had lied about knowing how to ride a bike and paid the price for doing so.

BREAKFAST DISHES, HYMNS, AND PRAYERS

One of the things I enjoyed most was helping wash breakfast dishes at my cousin Guy's house. Guy's father was my mother Erma's brother, and his mother was my Aunt Carrie. She was such a happy and vibrant person. Like my own new mother, Erma, she was so nice to me. She was everything a loving aunt could be—fun, patient, creative, and godly.

Some mornings, I washed pots and pans at Aunt Carrie's and she would whistle and sing some of her favorite hymns alongside of me. At some point, she would slip off to her bedroom and do what she did daily—get down on her knees and pray for missionaries, our church, and her family and ours. She closed her bedroom door so she could pray out loud, and I do mean she prayed loud! There was no question heaven heard her many requests, which most often were for others rather than herself.

I do not know if the activity in heaven ever stops, but if it does, it was undoubtedly to listen to my Aunt Carrie's latest requests bellowed out from her bedroom.

AUNT CARRIE'S POWERFUL PRAYER

I often sat in a woven chair outside of Carrie's bedroom and listened to her pray. The way she prayed sounded like she had a direct phone line to God. Prayers for me to that point in my life were something to memorize not to actually mean. Her prayers seemed so different than that. They were so personal and real. I started realizing she actually believed what she was saying.

After praising God, Aunt Carrie would plead, knock, and even pound on heaven's door with requests. One day, I heard her call out my name as she was praying. I was so surprised, I fell off the chair! Aunt

Carrie heard the noise and flew out her bedroom door to see what happened. She quickly realized I had been eavesdropping on her conversation with God. Aunt Carrie didn't waste the moment. She said, "Agnes, you will get saved, give your life to Jesus, and marry a preacher!" She delivered her announcement in her no-questions-asked tone of voice.

Embarrassed, I didn't know how to respond. "Oh, I'm so sorry, Aunt Carrie," I said, "You startled me!" With that, I turned and ran home. I was fast, but I couldn't outrun God. As I ran through garden after garden toward home, this thought kept sprinting around my head: *What if she really has heard from God and that's my life's calling?*

TEN-FINGER PRAYER PAUSE:
LEARNING TO PRAY

Someone asked me recently, "Where did you learn to pray?" My answer was "by watching others who loved Jesus pray." Ironically, I had no idea what it meant to really pray when I left the orphanage. That changed when my aunts and uncles (who became my moms and dads) began modeling prayer for me. They did so, not in a classroom, but in their everyday life. While I didn't know exactly what was happening when they closed their eyes and seemingly talked to God, I knew they were trustworthy people. It was trust that led me to believe that if prayer was important to them, it must be important. Their witness made it possible to trust God's *with-ness.*

Without a doubt, the person God used more than anyone to teach me about prayer in my younger days was Aunt Carrie. She didn't set out to teach me anything. In fact, she didn't even know I was listening for the longest time. When I listened to her pray, I sensed God's power and presence. I knew she meant every word she prayed. It was so personal too. She was actually having a conversation *with* God. Her prayers were such a wonderful mystery. Her prayers didn't make me pray—they invited me. I wanted to talk with God the way she did. And in time, I did.

* * *

MORE LOVE TO GO AROUND, RONNIE ARRIVES

By now, I had a wonderful sense of environmental stability, safety, protection, provision—and best of all, belonging—with this precious couple so clearly devoted to being my new parents. They also adopted another child into our family about a year later. His name was Ronald. Ronald also had a history of being unloved and abandoned. It seemed God had given my parents an almost bottomless well of compassion and love for hurting children. Their constant and selfless love contributed greatly to the healing of my broken heart.

A CONCERNING CALL FROM RUBY

Not long after Ronnie's arrival, trouble came knocking and challenged my new family. Uncle Archie got the call just after breakfast one morning. It was from my blood sister, Ruby. She sounded worried. Uncle Archie furrowed his brow as he held up the phone so we all could hear the conversation.

"My father has found me and wants to know if I know the location of Agnes," Ruby said.

My new mother swallowed hard and looked away.

"Ruby, so nice of you to call us and let us know," we heard Uncle Archie say.

Ruby expressed her fear and concern. "Father was asking a lot of questions," she said. "I just thought you would want to know."

"Ruby, again thank you for letting us know. We will be praying for your safety," Uncle Archie assured her.

Uncle Archie knew my father was a man capable of selling his own flesh and blood. That meant he was likely capable of almost anything.

As Uncle Archie hung the phone up, the room remained silent. All eyes were on him.

Worry lines reappeared on his forehead. "I wonder why he wants to know about Agnes," he shared. "It can't be for any good reason."

Aunt Erma stood wiping her hands on a linen towel by the kitchen counter. "I don't like this at all," she stated, "I really don't."

HOME BY ANOTHER WAY: FLINT

Gently tapping his hand on the table, Uncle Archie was deep in thought as he began forming a plan.

"We need to move from here as quickly as possible for Agnes' sake," Uncle Archie announced. "My brother in Flint has been telling me about a job opening there. We don't have money for gas (Flint was 200 miles away), so I am going to hitchhike there first thing tomorrow morning. Start packing, everyone! We are leaving as soon as we can. And why not? I make only a dollar a day at this fruit farm. I know the job in Flint pays a lot more."

Uncle Archie's determination offered a glimmer of hope to us all. The look on Aunt Erma's face changed from worry to affirmation. She knew he was right. We needed to get out of town and do so quickly.

Uncle Archie was true to his word. As the sun kissed the horizon the next morning, Uncle Archie was packing a small suitcase with clothes. After a light breakfast, he kissed Aunt Erma goodbye and headed down the driveway to the road that led to the main highway. In those days it was safe to pick up hitchhikers. In fact, it was considered a neighborly thing to do.

So Uncle Archie began his quest. The next morning—a full 24 hours later—we heard from Uncle Archie. He called to let us know us he had arrived in Flint.

A few days later, Uncle Archie returned. When I saw him coming down the road, I ran out to meet him at the end of the driveway. We hugged each other tightly. The smile on his face told me everything I needed to know: his trip was a success! We were already packed and ready to go. We knew we needed to move quickly before my birthfather could find us.

Soon, the car was loaded and ready for the journey. It was jammed from floor to ceiling with packed suitcases, boxes of sheets, and a few pots and pans that jangled here and there. We had little time to say goodbye to the neighbors. That was sad but not all bad. No one really knowing when we left or where we were heading; that added an extra layer of protection for our family.

A few relatives managed to gather in the driveway to say their farewells. It was a bittersweet moment for all. "Please pray, Carrie, for us to make it all the way to Flint in our old jalopy," said my Aunt Erma.

"You have my promise," said Aunt Carrie. "I will be in prayer this entire week for your safe arrival." Aunt Carrie's spoke with confidence and her face reflected a certain peace and assurance that could only come from a woman daily engaged in praying for others.

Just before the car began to pulled away, Aunt Carrie looked at me through the rolled down back window. Winking at me, she said, "Agnes knows she can count on my morning prayers."

I blushed momentarily as I remembered the day she had caught me listening outside her bedroom door. It was our secret, and my Aunt Carrie, always gracious and kind, was determined it would remain that way.

HIGH SCHOOL YEARS AND THE BEST MOM EVER

Our sudden move to Flint occurred just in time for the beginning of my high school years. At Flint Technical High School, I made many wonderful friends. We began attending a loving church. The neighbors were so kind and helpful to us. But the best thing for me was having such a loving mother.

The years of cruel neglect at the Good Will Farm followed by the years of inhumane treatment at Holy Family Catholic Orphanage slowly began to fade away.

"Does it feel awkward and a little unreal to call your Aunt Erma, your mother?" asked my new friend, Ruth.

Her question was easy to answer, "Not at all! She is the only real mother I've ever known. She's as much a mother to me as my brother Ronnie and I are children to her."

Just to say the word "mother" had been so foreign to me for so many years. To a little girl who had known so many forced separations, rancid infirmary rooms, cruel child-labor chores, days and nights of inadequate food and clothing, ridiculous rules, and senseless beatings—to have a mother who truly loved and cherished me at last was a profound joy I could not then, and even today, put into words.

THINGS MONEY CAN'T BUY

Aunt Erma, now "Mother," never had much in the way of material goods. No one did in those days of stock market crashes and dust bowls. But what she gave to me was much more valuable than what money could buy.

For starters, Mom maintained a Christian atmosphere in our home. Like a watchful mother hen hovering over her beloved chicks, she kept a close eye on the books we read and the radio programs we listened to.

It didn't stop there. She closely monitored the things we discussed at the table at night and how we treated one another during the day, steadfastly refusing to allow unkindly comments or gossip in our home. Mother was truly an extraordinary woman. She was loved and appreciated by her family, neighbors, and many friends. Because of her loving heart and firm code of conduct, I was given the security of knowing I was loved. I never resented a single rule.

GRADUATION: BRIGHT FUTURE, OLD FEELINGS

My closest high school friend in those days was a girl named Patsy Sullivan. Patsy and I loved to talk about the days behind us and the ones ahead as we walked home from school. A third friend, Dorothy Mettie, whose family owned a drapery store, made up our triad of friends who shared many good times throughout high school.

As an 18-year old senior about to finish her high school career, it seemed like everyone around me knew what they wanted to do in the future... except me. It was frustrating to once again be different from the rest. Some were heading off to learn a trade, others to the military, and still others to work in their family business. A select few had announced they were going off to college. Silently, I wrestled with a feeling of emptiness in my heart as I had no plan after graduation.

Sadly, it was a familiar feeling—one that brought back the same painful emotion that gnawed at my heart during my darkest days at the orphanage. It just didn't make any sense to feel sad and out of place now that I had so many good friends and such a loving family. Yet, deep down something, or someone, was still missing in what seemed to be a never-ending, undefined "empty space" inside.

WANTING WHAT RUTH HAD

I noticed as our senior year came to a close that another one of my dear friends, Ruth, had begun to change in so many ways. For several years, she had been known as the "loose girl" and did her best to cover her emptiness and sadness with tons of makeup. One day, Ruth's heavy makeup suddenly disappeared. In its place was an indescribable new beauty. Her entire countenance and spirit were changed!

"Ruth, why do you seem so different? You're so calm, so joyful, so sure of your future?" I asked one day.

Her reply caught me entirely off guard, "That's because I'm trusting in Jesus Christ for my salvation. My entire life—my past, present, and future—I've given to Him."

I stood there speechless. I knew my mother and father were devout followers of Jesus. Somehow, I had always thought that was something for adults. *But I'm just a teenager*, I thought.

Yet, here Ruth was explaining an amazing change God had worked in her life that was evident to everyone.

"Agnes, Jesus loves us and sacrificed His life for me and you," she smiled. "He died on the cross to cover the penalty for all my sins. I feel clean for the first time, completely loved and accepted by Him. I have peace, I'm loved, and I have great hope."

I could see the change in Ruth, and I wanted what she had. God used her example and testimony to awaken a need in my life I had sensed for a long time. It would be just a little while longer before I would have my own life transformational experience with Jesus. And Ruth was one of the beautiful seeds God planted in my life to get me there.

GRADUATION, GRATITUDE, AND THE GOODNESS OF GOD

Ruth, Patsy, Dorothy, along with myself and many other friends graduated from Flint Technical High School in 1948. The war was over, the soldiers had returned home, factories were beginning to hire again, and the car industry in Flint and Detroit was booming. The future looked bright again for many living in the United States after so many years of hardships caused by the Great Depression and World War II.

As I prepared to walk across the stage and receive my diploma on graduation day, there were two other high schools, Central High School and Northern High School, that joined us for the ceremonies. We gathered in the Flint Atwood Stadium for our last time together as high school classmates. Flint Atwood Stadium was an impressive structure built in 1929 for just such special events. It was used often for football games, band concerts, and graduations such as mine. It was thrilling to look up into the stands and see hundreds, if not thousands, of people waving and smiling down on us.

The printed program indicated to everyone that I was graduating with "high honors" from high school. In fact, I was one of five students chosen as "Most Likely to Succeed."

Who would have ever guessed a little girl with just three dresses and two pair of shoes, who didn't even know the exact year of her birth, would one day be recognized and honored for her academic achievement, much less voted "Most Likely to Succeed" in front of an entire stadium?

As the high school bands began to play the regal, "Pomp and Circumstance," I looked up from my row of chairs and saw my mother, father, and brother (Ronnie) standing in the audience. At that moment, my heart seemed like it would burst from the debt of gratitude I owed them for all the love and joy they lavished on me over the years.

My mind raced back to age thirteen when I came to live with my parents. Times were hard in those days. They did not have to take me in, but they did. Because of their unselfish love and unconditional acceptance, they took on the heavy responsibility of raising a teenager. They gave me the priceless gift of being my parents. I also had the opportunity to grow up with my younger brother, Ronnie. There may have been wealthier people in the stands that graduation day; but in my heart, I knew I was the richest girl in the entire stadium.

My parents lovingly cared for me. They were gentle, honest, understanding, and true. They gave me something I had once thought was reserved only for the lucky and the strong. They gave me the gift of knowing I belonged somewhere and to someone who wanted me. Let me plead with you to never take such a precious gift for granted. For me, having a family was the greatest joy I had ever known.

GOD AND THE IMPOSSIBLE: COLLEGE

What happened next in life was something I thought would never be possible. But once again, God made a way when there was no way. I was going to college! I applied, was accepted, and enrolled at the University of Michigan at Flint. To save money, I completed my first two years of studies while living at home.

GOD AND HIS GREAT GIFT: SALVATION

During my second year of college, my father brought home a flyer about a Native American Chief who was going to be speaking at an itinerant tent meeting. Since I was partly Native American, he was pretty sure I would want to attend.

My father was right. I did want to go. But as the day of the event approached, I became terribly ill. My father, knowing my deep desire to attend, wrapped me up in a blanket and managed to get me there. As the Chief spoke, my heart burned within me. Like an arrow shooting straight at me, the Chief said, "You can have what I've got—a relationship with God through Jesus! You can have it!"

The next few moments would forever change my life. My father helped me get to the front of the tent where my soul and physical body were instantly healed. My illness was gone. I had been given a new beginning! I now knew exactly what my friend, Ruth, had sought to describe to me in high school. Indescribable peace and joy flooded my soul! The God-shaped hole in my heart inside was now filled. I was whole, healed, and set free—ready to live out my days with a heart burning for others to know Jesus and the life and purpose He daily gives.

* * *

TEN-FINGER PRAYER PAUSE:
SALVATION PRAYERS

"God, whatever needs done in my life—only you can do it. I surrender my way and my will. I'm tired of running the show. Forgive me for all the ways I've offended you, others, and have made a mess of things in my own life. Come, Jesus, you take the reins. Please rescue me and be the Master of my life." That's the essence of a salvation prayer. It's certainly what I desired God to do the day I entered the tent. Truthfully, I don't know exactly what words I prayed that day. Not really knowing how to pray, I repeated what the Chief said. What I do know is that God heard every word and did a miraculous thing in my heart and life right then and there.

You don't have to pray the perfect prayer either. You need only to pray a most sincere prayer in asking Jesus to come into your life, forgive your sins, and make you clean and whole. If you ask Him, He will. I promise! Not because I say so, but because God does. You can trust God when He says, "For everyone who calls on the name of the Lord will be saved" (Romans 10:13). *Everyone* includes you! If you haven't asked Jesus to be your Savior and Lord, do it today. Do it right now! It's the greatest and best decision you can and will ever make!

GOD MAKES A WAY FOR MARION

Not too long after my salvation experience, something quite unexpected occurred. Word got out about "this young gal" who had just trusted Christ alone for her salvation.

Just before my junior year of college, we arrived home from a vacation, and there was a letter waiting for me from Marion College in Indiana. The letter simply stated an anonymous person was pleased to hear I had become a Christ-follower and wanted to pay for me to attend college there. I read the letter, then read it a second time. I simply could not believe it; I was about to become a student at Marion College (known today as *Indiana Wesleyan University*).

That fall, my parents loaded the car with suitcases and drove south from Michigan to Marion, Indiana. I was officially a college student at a four-year institution. As my father and others helped carry my belongings into the dormitory, I could not help but remember the days when all my earthly possessions could fit in an A&P grocery bag. Could this all be happening to me or was it only a dream?

This much I knew, it was God who provided the generous scholarship to Marion College that paid for all my classes and dormitory fees. I was where God wanted me to be.

4

MARION TO MARRIAGE

SADIE HAWKINS DAY

Soon I was settled into college life and loving every minute of it. Still, transition is transition, and I continued to search for my place and to know where I belonged in this whole new world. I learned throughout the years that a change in scenery doesn't mean that all the things you've been dealing with and overcoming your whole life instantly disappear.

In those early days at Marion College, during the colorful fall season, they had a special "Sadie Hawkins" Day. On this one day of the year, a race was held where the girls were allowed to chase after the boys. If they "caught" their sought-after prize, the two would spend the entire day together.

[The following is an adapted and personalized version of my experience one Sadie Hawkins Day from the book Forge by Fire: Making Intimacy with God your Greatest Gift, written by my son, Dwight, along with my nephew, John Boyd. If you'd like to buy the book or learn more about the ministry of Forge, go to ForgeForward.org.]

Near the Sadie Hawkins Day starting line a soft-spoken exchange took place.

"Psst. Are you going to run?" a male student inquired. He had noticed I wasn't getting lined-up for the chase. "If you do run," he whispered and winked, "I'll let you catch me."

"I'm not running," I replied.

"Why not?" he asked.

"I have a heart problem."

It was untrue. My heart was fine, but it was the only on-the-spot excuse I could think of to avoid participating in this race already evoking more pain and risk than I wanted to face.

I'd already been socially tagged as a worldly misfit. The race proved only to provoke the feelings of undesirability I was carrying.

Un-valuable and *undesirable* had marked my life far too many years. The day my mother dropped me off at the orphanage and never was my "mom" again, left an indelible imprint on my soul. Never a single word of love. Never an "I wonder how you're getting along?" Never a visit, a postcard, a call, a Christmas gift, or a personalized birthday card. Never having known the comfort or joy of being physically held or comforted by the one who gave her birth.

My growing-up years taught me all too well and all too often the disappointment of chasing but never catching, of waiting but never being found. Wanting to be desired and chosen, but instead experiencing the pain of people saying or indicating "not her," left me wondering how I could ever assume a position on the *chaser* side of such a quest.

That's why I didn't feel like running the race that day. Instinctively, what I felt most like was running away.

All those years in the heartless, industrial-like dormitory setting of the orphanage pushed me toward acquiring survival skills that would help me endure a life of never feeling personally wanted or valued. So, I feigned a heart problem. It was the fastest, most easily understood, and socially acceptable way out of participating that day.

In truth, my excuse wasn't far off. I did have a heart problem. My heart had been wounded and weakened from the days of the orphanage to my arrival at this small, conservative college. Family-less in one setting, a misfit in the other.

My past and present left me confused about any situations where being chosen would naturally leave some unchosen. Someone not being chased after or another not being caught didn't sit well with me—even if this was just a single-day, Sadie Hawkins event.

My mind raced back to when I was thirteen. I had been selected and checked out for an exploratory date weekend by a couple. I didn't really know the purpose of our meeting, but I remember being so hopeful that maybe somehow, some way, this was my chance to be adopted. The husband and wife couldn't agree on me as a mutual ongoing choice, however, so they returned me to the orphanage late on a Sunday evening. Yet another overlooked and undervalued attack on my heart.

Feeling different than all those standing in the lines of chasees and chasers, I again heard a kind and interested male voice calmly say, "Psst. Just say, 'Stop,' and I'll let you catch me."

There was no confusion on his side of the line. He'd noticed me from a distance for a while and wanted to spend time with me. He saw me as a valuable prize worth pursuing. He also believed he had some value I might benefit from and enjoy as well. That's why he was nearly begging me to run—to take even just one step—in his direction. He wanted to be caught, and he wanted *me* to catch him.

Isn't that just like God's heart-desire after us? He invites you and me to "seek, thirst after, run, come close" to Him. Why? Because He wants to be found. In fact, He promises to be!

Despite any past or present experiences that have left you confused and heartbroken as someone overlooked or undervalued, isn't it worth the risk to pursue the God who says, "Run after Me and I'll let you catch Me"?

Your intentional pursuit of God may just change everything! It did for me that day. We started running and I yelled to Dave, "Stop," and he did. I smile every time I think about it—I almost ran over him. He really wanted me to catch him! And I did catch him. And he caught me.

— *Forged by Fire: Making Intimacy Your with God Your Greatest Gift*

NEW BEGINNINGS WITH DAVE, MARION, AND GOD

Dave's interest for me began ever so cautiously. We often reminded each other we were just friends. That suited me just fine for the time being. Why should I worry about boys when I was having the time of my life at college?

As the autumn months wore on, the bright green cornfields of Indiana "fired" as the farmers refer to it. The green stalks slowly took on a golden color as they ripened for harvest. The smell of burning leaves, the crisp morning air with just a hint of chill, combined with the ever-changing colors of the towering oak trees on campus, made even walking to class a joyous experience.

Even better, this was a place where God was becoming more and more real to me. Life at the orphanage taught me to believe religion was mainly about keeping a set of rigid rules and attending church each morning and evening. My time at college was teaching me my relationship with God was about so much more.

God was now someone I could meet with daily, and *personally*, in prayer and Bible study. I could experience His presence in worship in chapel and listen to challenging sermons. I could see His love at work in my kind friends and caring professors. I realized at last knowing God is about a relationship rather than rule-keeping.

Oh, how I hoped all the other young boys and girls I had met at the orphanage, who would stand in their ragged clothes and worn-out shoes, eyes filled with sadness and fear from years of abandonment and abuse, could meet the same loving and caring Jesus I had met! The Jesus who said in the Bible, "Let the little children come to me…"

I prayed for them to receive the miracle I had experienced when my loving relative came looking for me. If only they could have heard the same words that changed my life forever, "Agnes, come down. There's someone here to meet you."

God was surely blessing me in these days. I was now living in a near idyllic setting at college, exploring new subjects, making new friends, and sitting under the wisdom of godly professors. Still, I could not get the faces of my own family out of my mind, nor my friends at the orphanage, and especially Pansy. I wanted for them what God had so graciously done for me.

That's why I've continued to keep all my past friends in my heart regardless of the years or the passing decades. I've prayed for them that God would perform a miracle in their lives as He had in mine. And because I know heaven is a real place, I believe I will see sweet Pansy again—this time with no cruelty, tears, or parting. We will no longer be orphans but sons and daughters of God. Because of the finished work of Jesus Christ on the Cross and His shed blood for each and all, we will all be God's children, adopted into His forever family.

DAVE'S OPENING OVERTURE: A CONCERT

One bright fall day as I walked down the long brown tile corridors of a classroom building complete with glazed windows on the doors and open transoms above to circulate the air, my eye caught someone heading toward me. As I balanced my books in one arm and my purse in the other, Dave walked up to me. I could see on his face a hint of worry or perhaps nervousness.

"Agnes," he hesitated, "I was wondering if you would… what I mean is would you consider… well, I thought maybe you would go to the concert with me? It's nothing personal you understand. It's just I need someone to go with me… as a friend… it's okay if you say no."

As his nervous eyes glanced at the floor, I could not help but feel sorry for him. He waited for me to answer. Female intuition told me to make him wait just a moment or two longer before I answered.

"Sure, why not?" I shrugged my shoulders. "We're just friends."

"You will? Oh, Agnes, that's great. I mean… thank you! I mean… I'll pick you up at five."

Both of us knew there was more behind his request and more behind my saying yes than we were willing to admit. But Dave was right, it was better to take things slowly. If there was any girl on earth who had learned to be cautious with her heart, it was me. Without a hint of self-pity, I could honestly say I had known enough heartbreak for two lifetimes, if not three.

The concert that evening, far from being the finale to our relationship, proved to be the opening overture.

I would watch from the vantage of the big picture window in our dormitory on the second floor of Teter Hall for Dave to walk up to the door. My close friend, Helen Sparks, helped me watch from our perch and was the keeper of my school secrets. The main lunchroom was located in the basement of my dormitory, so my second-floor window was a convenient lighthouse. Each time I saw him approach, my heart would skip a beat. While there were dozens of other handsome and eligible young men on campus, I ignored them all. I only had eyes for Dave.

VANILLA ICE CREAM

As I said, our dates in those days were simple fun. Neither of us had money for restaurants downtown. Instead, we would walk hand in hand two blocks from campus to buy an ice cream cone. In those days you could get a single cone of vanilla ice cream for the whopping price of five cents a scoop. Unfortunately, vanilla was the only flavor they offered. Doubly unfortunate, for some reason vanilla ice cream never agreed with me.

I certainly didn't want to hurt Dave's feelings, whose chivalry would not allow me to ever pay. Instead, as Dave chatted with other students who came to get ice cream too, I would quietly place my cone in the garbage can and softly float my napkin over it. If he ever caught me doing so, he never said.

CAMPUS FUN

At times we jokingly referred to Marion College as SMU—South Marion University. In reality, we knew we had little in common with large universities like the one in Texas. We were a small Christian college located in a small-town far from big city lights and huge football stadiums. There wasn't much going on, so we had to make our own fun.

Dave played basketball for our college team, and I was a cheerleader.

That meant we saw each other at every game. Every time he sank a shot or stole the ball from a competitor, he would steal a glance in my direction to see if I had been watching. I would smile at him and he would grin from ear to ear, then turn and pick up the pace. There isn't a man alive who doesn't want to impress his girl and have her cheer him on.

TRAVELING MUSIC MINISTRY

Dave and I shared a mutual love of music and ministry. So much so, Dave created and hand picked a ministry team that represented our college at local churches on weekends. The Marion College Ministry Team members were Roland "Red" Conley, Don Dawalt, Chub and Loraine Weatherby, Eldine Landis, Gail Miller, Dave Robertson, and me. Instrumentally the team included a trumpet trio, vocal duet and quartet, and a pianist. David was in the trumpet trio, and he and I also sang the duets. Our job was to travel throughout the Midwestern states and conduct concerts and recruit students to attend our college.

We logged hundreds of miles performing at small churches in a seven-state region. Those long car rides together were far from monotonous. As we cruised by black and white dairy cows grazing in pastures, bright red barns with white trim, and picturesque old farmhouses with big front porches, all the magnificent scenery served to bond our hearts and lives.

Arriving at our church destinations brought even more excitement. Each church was an adventure. Some churches were newer, many were older. The older churches were often the ones with wool raised carpets and missionary maps adorned with yarn and pushpins. We ate countless casseroles and slices of cold Spam. For dessert, we often enjoyed Jell-O salads with carrot shavings mixed into the red gelatin and topped with a dollop of mayonnaise. For the most part, we ate quite well at the Sunday potluck dinners in church basements outfitted with metal folding chairs and white paper covered tables.

As for money, the Ministry Team took love offerings at churches to cover expenses. To be honest, the offering plates often contained more *love* than *money*. But by God's gracious provision, our expenses were always covered. Beyond that, several of us were being prepared for a lifetime of service in the local church. That was certainly true for Dave and me.

Even as Dave and I blended our voices together in duets to sing old gospel favorites such as, "The Old Rugged Cross," and "Just as I Am," we learned at the same time to blend our hearts in worship and service to God's people as we traveled throughout Ohio, Indiana, Iowa, Michigan, Wisconsin, Kentucky, and western Pennsylvania.

DAVE'S PASTORAL CALL

Dave was a music major and a talented one at that. He could play any number of musical instruments beyond the ones I mentioned. During Christmas break Dave went home for the holidays and received a most unexpected gift. Among all the lights and traditional Christmas music he loved so much, God spoke to his heart in a direct and powerful way. The present God gave Dave that December was a call to be a pastor.

When he returned to campus in January, there was a new resolve and determination on his face and in his heart. He knew God wanted him to serve as a minister of the gospel. He was to spend his life preaching the Word of God and caring for the hearts of people. Given Dave had grown up in a pastor's home, I suppose it should not have come as a complete surprise.

Yet, far from clutching onto his father's coattails, this was Dave's call. Some say if you can do anything else with your life then being a preacher, you should. Pastoring outside God's call is a miserable place to be.

Pastoring is tough business. Contrary to some popular opinion, pastors work a lot harder than one day a week! The ministry is often difficult, and at times, a heart-breaking endeavor. While most sheep love their shepherd, there will always be wolves among them. While most affirm and pray for their pastor, there will always be those who criticize, gossip, and cause division. While all Christians experience suffering from following Christ, pastors and other church leaders live with an unusual level of spiritual warfare. It's as if they have a target painted on their back—because they do. As the Scriptures teach, if you strike the shepherd, you can scatter the sheep (Zechariah 13:7). That's why our Enemy often takes special aim at pastors and their families.

Yet, pastoring is also a wonderful and magnificent work. It is life's highest privilege to preach and teach the Word of God. There is no more thrilling experience than to lead people to a saving relationship with Christ. To endure in such a great work, you must know you are called there by God. That calling will sustain you through the good and bad of life in the ministry.

God specifically called Dave by name to surrender his life to fulfill the purpose God had for him. God told him how he would spend his life, and Dave knew he must obey. What's more, Dave wanted to. He desired to love, serve, and please Jesus more than anything else in life.

MARRIAGE IMMINENT, DAVE MEETS MY FAMILY

In our church tradition, engagement rings and jewelry were frowned upon as "too worldly." While we didn't have a tangible gesture of our intentions, little by little Dave began to talk about the future as "we" and "us." At first, he was rather casual about it. Perhaps he was just testing the water. Over time, he became emboldened to the point where he treated it as just a matter of fact—we *would* get married. He assumed I felt the same. He was right.

As the dark snows of winter melted and formed puddles and streams in the streets of Marion, spring was evident. Spring seemed like the right time and season for Dave to meet my family. As the Lord would have it, our ministry team traveled northward to my home church, Chevrolet Avenue Church, in Flint, Michigan. Now a booming car town with factories working three shifts, Flint was heading into its heyday as a leader in the auto industry. Now that better times were here, the factory assembly lines would churn out new cars 24-hours a day to satisfy America's love affair with the automobile.

The Chevrolet Church (an appropriate name for a church in the heart of Flint), was started in the early 1940s by many family members with the last name of Nichols. Many other families eventually joined them as most men now had jobs in the factories or businesses related to it. I was so excited for my immediate family and my church family to meet Dave. I was thrilled to introduce this very handsome, musically talented, and godly fiancée God had gifted to me. It was amazing to think God had given someone who loved not only me, but my family, my church, and my Lord.

Though I did not often let my thoughts go there, I could not help but wonder how my mother's life, the life of my blood brothers and sisters, and my own life would have been different if my mother had only married a man such as Dave. What if, instead of marrying a man willing to sell his family for money and his addiction, my mother had married someone willing to lay down his life for his family and Lord? What if my father had turned to Christ with his pain and sin instead of to liquor and violence? Those are questions I have had to leave with Jesus. I know one day all of life's mysteries and sorrows will be solved when we see Him face to face.

I was so happy to see my dad. I was so proud of him. He once rebuilt our garage by tearing down a friend's four-car garage and making us a new two-car garage out of the same lumber. My parents, due to necessity, were very thrifty. They were always repairing or improvising to make do with what we had, which proved to be helpful life lessons for me.

When I spotted my little brother Ronnie on the front porch, I ran up and hugged him tightly. He had grown so much even since Christmas. Ronnie followed Dave and I around all weekend, and I was glad to call him my brother.

My mom and dad welcomed Dave immediately into their hearts. They could see the joy he had brought into my life, and that's all they needed. Mom went all out to shower Dave with her delicious meals. Her legendary fried chicken and meatloaf left him pushing away from the table with arms held up in surrender.

She sent Dave back to campus with a big box of her extra special chocolate chip cookies. You know, the kind where the chocolate melts on your fingertips if you don't eat them right away. If the way to a man's heart is through his stomach, she had all but taken Dave hostage.

PROPHETIC WORDS COME TRUE

As our days at my home grew to a close, I could not help but remember the prophetic words my Aunt Carrie had spoken to me when I was a girl. She had predicted not only would I get saved one day, but I would also become a pastor's wife. Given her life as a prayer warrior, I have little doubt she helped pray me into God's Kingdom and Dave into my life. According to the Bible, the test of a prophet is if their words come true. While Aunt Carrie would have strongly denied she was any sort of a prophetess, at the same time, she knew when she had heard from God. And, as far as she was concerned, the matter was settled.

MY TURN TO MEET DAVE'S FAMILY

Now it was Dave's turn to plan a trip to Pennsylvania and introduce me to his family. His parents pastored a small church in Erie, Pennsylvania, just over the river from Youngstown, Ohio. They say meeting your future in-laws for the first time is like being a long-tailed cat in a room full of rocking chairs. While I was excited to be introduced to Dave's family, I had a mild case of the jitters. Would they like me? Would I make a good first impression? Would they think I was good enough for their Dave?

We drove the long trip from northern Indiana to western Pennsylvania in Dave's secondhand "college car." I was so exhausted from finals week and my campus job; I badly needed some sleep. I asked Dave to please wake me up about one hour before we arrived. I would need time to freshen up, do my hair, and make myself presentable.

It was a rainy night, the kind where your headlights are absorbed into the dark asphalt. Dave was so intent on staying safely on his side of the road in the dark and rain, he forgot to wake me up. I remember him gently shaking me and saying, "Agnes, wake up. We're here." The next thing I knew I spotted his mom and dad running out of the parsonage toward the driveway to greet us.

I glanced into the rearview mirror and felt like fainting. It was too late. There was no time left to undo the damage to my hair from sleeping with my head on Dave's shoulder. With one side flattened down a little and the other fluffed up... well, I guess they would get to know the real me right from the start.

For our first meal together, Dave's mom made a wonderful beef stew with canned vegetables from last summer's garden. The stew was flavored just right, the vegetables soft and chewy, and the beef melted in my mouth. I realized she too wanted to make a good first impression.

"Please, have some more," she said as she ladled another helping to my bowl.

David's younger sister, Elizabeth, or "Betty" as the family called her, generously gave up her bedroom for me. She grinned as she knelt down on the floor with her ear pressed hard against the furnace register. Through the open duct she could hear everything her parents were saying downstairs. Like a telegraph operator receiving vital news from the front lines, she dutifully repeated to me everything Dave's mom and dad were saying.

"I think they like you," she whispered. "They say you are polite, well-mannered, and think you have a nice smile."

It was all great fun, but my uneasy conscience wouldn't let me enjoy the eavesdropping (even though I was dying to know what they thought of me).

The next day went well with his family, and so did the next and the next. I knew Dave loved me with such an unconditional love. His acceptance of me was wholehearted and complete—my painful past and all.

CHILDHOOD TRAGEDIES, GOD'S TRIUMPHS

Still, Dave and I both knew there was one thing that could possibly turn things sour. There was something we were going to have to tell his parents sooner or later. We spent several hours wondering how his parents would react when we told them that I was adopted.

Finally, Dave just blurted it out one evening, "Dad and Mom, I want you to know Agnes was adopted." Dave placed the metaphorical elephant squarely in the middle of the living room.

Silence. For a moment it seemed all the oxygen had just left the room. I began studying the faces of Dave's mother and father. Were they shocked? Upset? Disappointed?

I held my breath as Dave's father was the first to speak.

His voice was gentle and reassuring, "Dave, there is something you need to know as well. We never told you this, but your mother was adopted as well."

Dave's dad reached over and took his wife's hand.

We both sat on the overstuffed couch in stunned disbelief. Now it was Dave's parent's turn to wonder how we would react to the news. Dave was quiet as he looked over to his Grandfather Verbridge who was seated in an easy chair across from us. It slowly dawned on Dave that his grandfather was not Dave's flesh and blood relative. Holding the weight of that thought for just a moment, Dave decided the freshly delivered news didn't change anything. God had given him a loving and kind grandfather to grow up with and that's all that mattered.

The awkwardness in the room turned to relief as everyone smiled and nodded at one another. From that day onward, I felt loved by Dave's family in every way possible. Dave's mother and I now had a special bond between us. It was a bond we shared until her heavenly journey at age 93. We were twin adoptees, and that meant we understood, accepted, and loved one another in ways few daughters-in-law and mothers-in-law ever reach. Once again, God had worked everything out for me.

A HERITAGE OF PASTORS AND MINISTRY

I quickly became friends with Dave's two younger sisters, Phyllis, who eventually married Donald Boyd (a pastor and later a professor at

Asbury Theological Seminary in Kentucky), and Elizabeth, "Betty," who eventually married Pastor Bill Tice.

With the sweet smell of spring surrounding us, we sat evening after evening on the porch and listened to Dave's father, Pastor Dwight Robertson, tell stories from his life. Tragically, Dwight's own father had died in a mining accident. His father was in his early 50s and worked as an electrician in the coal mines when he suffocated from toxic air in the mine. Dwight was forced to support his mom and siblings by working in the same coal mines where his father died, along the Allegheny River in Templeton, Pennsylvania. People had to grow up fast in those days.

At age 25, Dwight was chosen as a delegate for the denomination's Annual Conference. That year, it was held in Sandy Lake, Pennsylvania. It was while he was there, he felt God called him into full time Christian ministry. When he got back home, he continued to work in the mines and pursued his ministry degree through correspondence courses.

His brother, Art Robertson, also became a pastor. One year, during the weeklong revival meeting at Pastor Art's church, he hired a song evangelist named Leona Verbridge to lead music. Her voice was lovely and her close walk with Christ was evident to Dwight. The second night of the meetings, his brother invited both Leona and Dwight to enjoy dinner at the parsonage after the service. It didn't take long until they fell in love. And that's the story of how Dave's father and mother met.

Besides making homemade soup for us on Saturday evening, Dave's mom also prepared a sumptuous meatloaf for Sunday Dinner. Dwight's parents did not like to work on Sunday. For them, Sunday was the Sabbath Day, a day to worship and rest, not work. So, they always cooked Sunday dinner the night before.

I remember Sunday morning there was a sweet presence of the Holy Spirit in the church service. After church, we enjoyed the meatloaf Dave's mom had prepared. It was the best I had ever eaten (besides my own mother's meatloaf, of course).

I told my twin-adoptee, mother-in-law-to-be what a great cook she was. I knew if her story was anything like mine, there may have been weeks, months, perhaps years where she never heard a kind word of appreciation. I was just making up for lost time with words that should have been constantly spoken over her life from the beginning.

DAVE PROPOSES

Before we left to head back to college, Dave summoned the courage to ask his dad what he thought about asking me to marry him? Dave's dad rubbed his jaw and thought for a moment. His contemplative look turned into a smile, "Well, you two are together most of the time now," he said, "so you might just as well get married. How about next summer?"

I guess Dave's sister, Betty, had heard right the first night she listened through the floor furnace register. His parents did approve of me.

Dave and I piled our things into his car and drove back to college. Not many days passed by before Dave asked me to marry him. It was not a formal or dramatic proposal like you might see in the movies. No getting down on one knee, tearfully pledging his eternal fidelity and undying love, or popping open a black box with a blinding diamond inside (our church tradition at the time frowned on wearing rings, even wedding bands). Dave's proposal was a sincere and straightforward question, "Agnes, will you marry me?"

"Yes," I said, with great delight and no reservation.

WEDDING BELLS AND BLESSINGS

We were married the next summer, June 28, 1952, in my parent's living room in Flint, Michigan.

When my Aunt Crystal (Nichols) showed up for the wedding, she asked me, "What are you wearing for your wedding dress?"

"I am wearing my best Sunday dress," I said.

"No," said Aunt Crystal, "that just won't do. Get in my car, we're going shopping. Let's go find a brand-new, white wedding suit for you."

My wedding corsage showcased pansies, my favorite flower. I had a little part of my best friend Pansy from the orphanage with me on my special day.

It was a very warm June day and there was no air conditioning. Our close family members fanned themselves and the children squirmed as they waited for me to walk in. As my father walked me into the living room, I remember how grateful I was for the security and stability he had brought into my life.

I could hardly believe this was happening to me. When I arrived in the room, all Dave and I could do was just gaze at one another as the pastor helped us recite our vows. Just as God had poured out His grace in sending Jesus into my life, that same grace had sent me this amazing man to be my life-long companion.

As we held hands and repeated our vows, I could only marvel at all that God had done in the two years since we had met for the first time. Not since the year I was rescued from the orphanage had so many wonderful things happened in my life in such a short time.

Our wedding reception was at a community center with an open invitation to family and friends. As we joined hands and sliced our five-layer wedding cake, so many joyous memories replaced the worn and tattered ones of growing up. Gone were the memories of a little girl who was left to cry herself to sleep every night, who held a solitary orange close to her heart as her friend, who was reminded time after time that no one would ever want her. Fresh and alive was the awareness of new memories being created. I was a bride who was greatly loved and honored, dressed in a beautiful white suit, surrounded by smiling friends and family, and now married to a man who had chosen a new name for me—a name he would call me for the rest of our lives.

Looking into my eyes, Dave gently whispered to me that wonderful wedding day, "Beautiful Agnes."

5

NEWLYWEDS

HONEYMOON HAVEN OR HEARTBREAK HOTEL?

There is a saying among pastors who take on a new church only to discover serious problems and immediate crises meeting them at the door on Day One. Pastors who experience such dynamics often say, "I never got a honeymoon."

The same could be said for my beloved Dave and me. We had made arrangements following our marriage ceremony and reception for an idyllic honeymoon at a pristine lake. What could be more secluded, ideal, and romantic, right? Well, here's the story of how Honeymoon Haven almost turned into Heartbreak Hotel.

My high school friend, Dorothy Mettie, made arrangements for us to use her family's lake home to spend a honeymoon week. While secluded, the lake wasn't far from Flint.

While Dave did not carry me across the threshold as some traditionally do, we arrived with a sparkle in our eyes and young, married passion in our hearts.

That night, as we settled into our upstairs room, something strange happened. First, the lights flickered. Then, they went completely off. Stranger still, the lights came back on again, then flickered, then went off. It's not how lights and electricity normally function—now or then. Making our hearts race even faster was a thud we heard coming from downstairs.

"Oh no, Dave," I cried. "Do you think they have found us?"

The "they" were my siblings and other relatives on my birth parent's side, chief among them—my estranged father. When they learned I was marrying a Protestant pastor, they became quite perturbed. Their anger ranged from "irritated" to "infuriated."

"I won't be coming to your wedding," one of my brothers announced. Another one told me, "If you go through with this, I'll no longer call you my sister!" And those were just the more magnanimous comments I received from some members of my birth family.

We had made a clean break from my father when we left the fruit farm in northern Michigan and moved to Flint. We were careful to keep our distance ever since. My greatest fear in getting married was that my biological father might somehow resurface in my life. So, when the strange things happened at the cabin, my first thought was that my father or birth brothers had found us.

Every flicker, every bump sent chills deeper down our spine. Fear continued to squeeze us tighter the longer it went. Our minds began playing worst-case scenarios. Maybe my birth father got word of where our wedding was and then followed us to the cabin? Maybe he was making his way into the cabin and up the stairs with the intent to exact his revenge. The thought of this violent alcoholic—a man willing to sacrifice one of his own children for another drink—standing outside our door, left me almost unable to breathe.

"I'll go downstairs and see what's going on," Dave bravely announced.

As he went down the stairs with flashlight in hand, I wondered if I would ever see my newlywed husband again.

After what seemed an eternity, he returned upstairs and reported, "I didn't see anyone. The door seems locked and shut."

I shared with Dave what I had been doing while he was away. "I found a doll bed filled with ceramic-headed dolls," I said. "I think one of those thrown hard and fast would make a great weapon." When fear grips you, all kinds of things seem rational at the time!

The day was wonderful but long, and we were exhausted. The evening drama served only to zap more energy from our reserve. So, we did the only thing we knew to do. Our hearts anxiously beating, we fell asleep in each other's arms.

The next morning, the same pattern repeated itself. The lights went on, then flickered, then off. The thuds continued their pattern in staccato fashion. With the whole day ahead of us, we knew sitting in fear and unsolved mystery wasn't what we wanted. We were done with it.

"That's it!" one of us said. "No more."

It was Sunday morning, so we decided to drive into town and call my parents. We told them of our nerve-wracking experiences and how we feared some family member was prowling about, intent on terrifying us, or at least ruining our honeymoon and week of serenity.

"Why don't you meet us at church this morning?" Dave's parents said.

That sounded like a much better use of our time. So, that's what we did. We headed to church. We were never so happy to see so many friendly faces.

"Maybe Mother and I will come up and join you," Dave's father said to us as we talked after the service. "That way, if anyone *is* up there, they'll have to deal with four people and not just two."

After some discussion, we decided that Dave's sister, Phyllis, and her boyfriend, Don Boyd, would also accompany my parents to stay at the cabin with us.

So, one day after our wedding we now had four other people joining Dave and myself for our honeymoon. We had five of us nestled in the cabin's lone bedroom upstairs and Don sleeping on the couch and keeping watch on the main floor. What a sight!

I need not explain that having six people including one's in-laws on a honeymoon is a less than ideal arrangement for two newlyweds! But, we did feel more safe and had a better chance of getting some rest and being alive at the end of the week.

Almost on cue, the lights and thumps once again began their menacing dance. Dave's father couldn't take it anymore. Armed with a flashlight and a determined glare to get the bottom of what was happening, he made his way to the level beneath the main floor—the boathouse.

After several minutes of poking around, Dave's father emerged from the cavern beneath and announced, "Well, I found the problem."

"What is it?" I asked in breathless anticipation.

"It's a short-circuit in the power cord that provides electricity to the cabin. Apparently, the wiring is old and somewhat frayed. That's why the power comes on and off."

"What about the bumps and thuds we hear all night?" Dave's mother asked.

Father just grinned. "That's the sound of the boats anchored downstairs bumping against the dock. Whenever the wind kicks up on the lake, the waves rock the boats and causes them to bump against the dock."

The investigation over and a sound explanations in hand, we let out a collective sigh of relief. Deranged, knife-wielding relatives weren't crouching in the basement waiting to pounce. Neither were they deviously terrifying us by flickering the lights and bumping the floor. The culprits were simply old wiring and rippling waves.

Since the "plus 4" reinforcements had so kindly and sacrificially driven a long way to help us, we invited them to stay with us through the next day. While a honeymoon with four extra guests might not be everyone's idea of the perfect honeymoon, we truly enjoyed their company.

OUR FIRST HOME AND LAST YEARS AT MARION

That fall, Dave and I returned to Marion College. One of the college professor's owned a home across the street from Teter Hall, the dormitory where I lived while Dave and I were dating. We rented an upstairs studio apartment in the professor's house for a whopping $37.50 a month. It was our first place together, and we loved it!

Dave had several more years left to finish his ministry degree. While he finished his studies, I worked with a securities company in downtown Marion and later took a job at a bank. During that time, we kept traveling and singing for the college most weekends with our friends on the ministry music team.

LIVING ON LOVE IN BLUE EYE, PENNSYLVANIA

When Dave graduated from Marion and received his ministerial degree in the spring of 1955, we were soon called to serve a small church in Blue Eye, Pennsylvania. The people who attended the church at Blue Eye were very poor. Our salary consisted of whatever people could put in the Sunday morning offering. That usually added up to something between $10 to $20 each week.

We lived on love and survived on what we got in the offering plate.

If we had one cup of coffee in the morning, we would leave a little in the bottom to add water for a second cup. We might have one chicken breast to fry and anything we could mix with water for soup.

One morning, Dave went out to empty the garbage behind the garage and spotted something growing in the ground that he hadn't noticed before. He crouched down and began to root among the weeds. He grasped a handful of what he thought were weeds and up came potatoes. We had hit gold! That encouraged us to try to plant a garden. Neither of us knew much about gardening. Yet, we dug straight rows with a hoe and lovingly dropped seeds in the ground. Soon tender green shoots began to appear. We were more than excited by the prospect of putting fresh, homegrown vegetables on our table.

BOVINE BURGLARS AND GOD'S APPOINTMENTS

Then, disaster struck. The neighbor's cows got out one day and found their way to our garden patch. As Bessie and Elsie grazed contently among the rows in our new garden, we watched our entire summer's effort become afternoon snacks.

But God is a good provider. As the saying goes: our disappointments often become God's appointments.

Sure enough, I called our neighbors and laughingly told them where their cows were feeding. Next thing we knew a huge hay wagon lumbered onto our property bulging with fresh corn, tomatoes, sweet potatoes, white potatoes, and ripe greens. One can only suppose the neighbors felt a little guilty about their cows eating the preacher out of house and home. They were so kind to make restitution for their bovine burglars. So great was the offering of food, we had enough left over to can some of the bounty for the coming winter!

Yes, times were hard. But the folks of Blue Eye loved us, and we loved them. And together, we all had what we needed.

MANNA FOR MISSIONARIES

One weekend, we had a missionary unexpectedly show up at our Sunday night service. Dave did the proper thing and invited him over for dinner.

There's a saying in ministry that "a pastor and his wife need to be ready for three things: to preach, pray, or die!" I can add a fourth imperative to that list... "and feed unexpected guests." We had nothing to feed the missionary, so I went down to the basement and found among the cobwebs a two-quart jar of what appeared to be some kind of vegetables. I cleaned up the jar and used them. I didn't know exactly what was in the jar or how old, but I added fresh butter. The missionary said they were delicious.

You might say we lived from hand to mouth in those days. But thank the Lord it was always *His* hand and our mouth!

MAKING KETCHUP

We did our best to make the most out of the resources we had in those days. One time, someone gave me a lot of tomatoes, so I decided to try my hand at making ketchup. I put them in a big pan, put the lid on, and cooked them. I took the lid off to stir them and steam burned me so badly that I had to go to the doctor. I never made ketchup again. Ever since that incident, we just buy it!

THE GROCERY STORE GOSPEL

There was a grocery story about two miles away from where we lived. It was popular with local residents and people would come far and wide to buy necessities. The owner was an older man and often a surly one at that. One day, we were out of bread and milk. Unfortunately, offerings at the church were sparse that month, and we had no money to buy the needed groceries.

I felt God was telling me to wait until later in the afternoon to go to the store. Throughout the years, I've learned to listen to such "promptings" from the Lord. I decided to go just before closing time. As the sun was setting, I heard the Lord say, "Agnes, go now." So, I immediately grabbed my things and went.

When I got to the grocery, I realized I was last customer in the store that day. Walking amid the aisles of stacked can goods and a pyramid of fresh fruit for sale, I spotted the owner sweeping the floor. He spotted me too. He knew I was the preacher's wife. As he swept, he struck up a casual conversation with me.

"I drive by your church every Sunday, and I've noticed more cars lately," he said.

I assumed this was his backdoor way of paying Dave and myself a compliment. Resting the broom against his apron, he stared out the window. His thoughts and words became more introspective.

"You know, I think about heaven. Is it a real place?" he said.

Never one to mince words when it comes to salvation, I looked at him straight in the eye and said "If you live a wicked life, you can't expect to go to heaven. God loves you unconditionally no matter what you have done. Repent of your sins and believe in Him for His forgiveness. Trust in Him and His shed blood alone for your salvation."

I don't regret what I said. Every word of it was true. What I did regret was that I didn't know at the time that the grocery store owner was considered by many "the town drunk!"

Well, that's all it took. He stood up from leaning on his broomstick and pointed toward the door.

"There's the door, you can use it," he said.

I did as he asked. As I opened the door to leave, the owner's voice suddenly softened.

"Wait a moment," he said, "Please come back."

For the next five minutes, he proceeded to go up and down the aisles and fill a grocery bag with all kinds of food items. He even gave us ice cream! (we hadn't had ice cream in a very long time). God is so good!

Several months later, the store owner was walking down by the railroad tracks and got fatally bitten by a snake. I often wondered if, in the 30 to 45 minutes he lay dying, he remembered what I told him about the gospel message. I sure hope he did.

6

BLUE EYE TO BARBERTON

PASTORAL LIFE AT BLUE EYE

We loved the people at Blue Eye. The church did the best they could to worship and serve the Lord. The pianist played the piano with two fingers. A quartet was any four people who happened to be singing at the same time. Our Sunday school teacher once taught a lesson on Jesus' words to Lazarus, "Come forth!" The teacher concluded, "Jesus couldn't say that today—Lazarus would be cleaned out [embalmed] already!"

The parsonage at Blue Eye was an old schoolhouse built during the Civil War (some 90 years earlier) when the local men headed off to such far-off places as Chickamauga, Chancellorsville, and Vicksburg. In the decades since the War Between the States, little upkeep had been done to the schoolhouse. As a result, the building had fallen into serious disrepair. We repurposed the old attic into a bedroom. When it rained, we would have to move our bed to avoid the steady dripping.

Yes, life at Blue Eye had its hardships and hangups. But God loved the people there and we loved them too. Loving God and people makes a pretty good life.

THE BIRTH OF OUR FIRST CHILD

Marcia Agnes, our first child and only daughter, was born in the fall of 1955. Dwight "Ike" Eisenhower was in the White House, bread cost a dime a loaf, and a once obscure boy from Mississippi, named Elvis, was becoming a household name (though not so much in our house).

GOD, OUR FAITHFUL PROVIDER

Looking back, the Lord provided for us so faithfully at Blue Eye. Dave was able to find extra work just when we needed it most. One particularly lean season, our cupboards nearly empty and the refrigerator housing little more than a light bulb and an ice cube tray, we got a call from a large church in the area. They heard about Dave's musical gifts and invited us to do the music for a revival. The revival lasted an entire week! Some might say, "What great luck!" but we would tell you that our Heavenly Father was demonstrating once again that He is Jehovah-Jireh, *The God Who Provides.* "So, Abraham called that place The Lord Will Provide. And to this day it is said, 'On the mount of the Lord it will be provided'" (Genesis 22:14). Today, now 70 years later, I continue to attest and proclaim, "Our God, Jehovah-Jireh, provides!"

TEN-FINGER PRAYER PAUSE:
PRAYERS FOR PROVISION

I learned early on in life that God is a faithful provider. That may seem a bit strange to hear considering my rough start. But that's precisely the point. God provided everything I *needed* when I needed it. Clothes, food, relationships, a divine rescue—all came just at the right time. That made it easier as time went on to look back and realize "God saw me through then, surely He'll see me through in this current situation." And God has— every time!

There have been countless times my hands have been raised in a 10-finger prayer posture saying something like, "Lord, the only way we'll have enough here is if you provide it, because we've done all we can do and all resources have been exhausted." And God comes through. He really does—not necessarily with the things we *want* but with all that we *need*. That's what God did for the Israelites in the desert (Exodus 16). He provided *manna*—exactly what they needed, not too much and not too little. And God supplied the Israelites their needed nutrition day after day for 40 years!

Because of God's ongoing faithfulness, I've continued to practice what the Apostle Paul called "being content in all circumstances" (Philippians 4:12). I've learned that God is enough. God's proved Himself time and again that He is dependable to supply all my needs, and always right on time.

God will do the same for you. Ask Him! If you don't know already, you'll soon learn—when the Lord is your Shepherd, you lack nothing you really need.

* * *

NEW BABY, NEW TOWN, NEW ASSIGNMENT

Two years later, our son Dwight was born. He turned over onto his belly in the hospital! That is quite a feat not usually accomplished until the age of six months. The doctor said, "He must be a very strong baby."

We received a call to serve a church in Loyal Oak, Ohio, a community 200 miles away. I was still recuperating in the hospital after Dwight's birth (in those days women stayed at least a week, sometimes two, after giving birth) when Dave packed up the house with Marcia.

Ten days later, Dave picked me up from the hospital and our young family moved to Barberton, Ohio (an adjacent town about a 10-minute drive from the Loyal Oak church).

As we left the hospital, the doctor paid a visit to my room and re-emphasized, "Dwight's already rolling over, so he's probably going to be a very busy baby. Just keep him dry and let him fuss," the physician advised. Did that physician ever get that one right!

LOYAL OAK, FAITHFUL GOD

Our new appointment was a basement church that attracted a lot of teenagers to the congregation. Many of the young people were amazing Christians. Many of the young women went on to marry preachers or full-time Christian workers. Several of the young men went on to become preachers themselves. They really cared for one another in their faith journey. For instance, I remember the boys made a pact with one another to only date Christian girls, and the girls in the church made a commitment only to date Christian boys. They both really wanted to love and please God more than anything.

I remember with great fondness putting on several concerts at the church. I would play the piano while Dwight and Marcia would have a great time in the nursery. We had such wonderful volunteers that helped out with the children.

One year during our annual Christmas program, we had a curtain strung across the stage prior to the opening of the pageant. When the curtain opened, there was a live Nativity scene with real people playing Joseph, Mary, and the shepherds.

Little Marcia's eyes grew wide as tea saucers. She suddenly jumped out of the lap of the lady who was holding her and darted down the middle aisle. She was a girl on a mission. She made her way to the platform and stared down into the manger. In shock and dismay, Marcia turned her gaze from the manger to the piano where I was seated. With great disappointment, she exclaimed, "It's just a doll!"

God didn't waste any opportunities with Marcia's curiosity and boldness—even at four-years old. More than once, Marcia could sense God calling people to the altar to commit their lives to Christ. So, she boldly led the way. She'd get out of her seat, be the first one down the aisle, and inevitably the altar would line up with people.

Miraculous answers to prayer happened as well at Loyal Oak. Once, we had a young mother in the church who was dying. She prayed and asked God for two more years so she could prepare her 14-year old daughter for adulthood and disciple her.

We prayed, and God answered her prayer. The mother lived exactly two years to the day of her prayer. In the time God granted the mother, the daughter grew in her love for the Lord and eventually became a missionary to wayward girls.

THREE'S A CHARM

While at Loyal Oak, God graciously added a third child to our family, another wonderful son, David.

We had many lovely memories of life in the beautiful second story apartment that was our home. We stayed at Loyal Oak for nearly 3½ years before we got a call from Sandy Lake Wesleyan Church in Pennsylvania. Their call and invitation to be their pastor prompted us to seek the Lord once again in discerning His Kingdom assignment for the next season of our lives.

As we prayed about it, God made it clear it was time to love people and serve His Kingdom in a new location. We would miss our time at Loyal Oak and the great group of teenagers we had come to love so much.

7

SANDY LAKE

SANDY LAKE CHURCH AND ZION

In September of 1960, we moved our growing family to Sandy Lake, Pennsylvania. Sandy Lake Church brought new challenges, adventures, and ways of doing things. It was there that I learned to play the organ. Worship was enhanced for families with children through the offering of a "cry room" in the rear of the sanctuary. The "cry room" was a glassed-in room where parents could hold their crying babies or antsy toddlers and continue to worship while giving their kids needed care. Plenty of volunteers helped out as well so that worship could be a pleasant and meaningful experience for everyone who attended.

The Sandy Lake Church had an additional church in the county, Zion Church. The two congregation partnership is what's called in church terms a "two-point charge." So, we actually pastored two churches at the same time. Zion was an old church next to a small cemetery where many former saints and pastors who had served the church were buried.

Zion Church had no inside plumbing, only an outhouse. The outhouse proved challenging during winter months. Having to walk out in the cold, remove winter clothes, re-dress, and return to the church in freezing or rainy weather wasn't much fun for anyone—young or old. To make matters worse, the church didn't have a heating system either. An old-fashioned pot belly stove was the single source of heat on a Sunday morning. Attendees would gather around the stove to keep warm. On colder Sundays, hymn-singing was accompanied by visible signs of people's breath as they sang.

THE OLD FARMHOUSE PARSONAGE

In time, Zion church decided to become its own congregation with its own pastor. Because the parsonage was owned by both congregations, the two churches decided to sell it and divide the assets. We were somewhat saddened by the decision. The parsonage was a lovely, old, country farmhouse at the top of the hill with a big front porch where the kids loved to play.

When the churches sold the parsonage, we moved temporarily down the hill into an old store building. We had some good times there. Dave's mother was living with us at the time, and we enjoyed that. She was a lot of fun, especially with our kids!

THE NEWLY CONSTRUCTED PARSONAGE

Splitting the assets of the old parsonage allowed the church to build a new one. Knowing we had temporary living conditions, the church got the new parsonage built as quickly as possible. It was beautiful! It had five bedrooms, two bathrooms, a big basement, and a two-car garage with an upstairs room. The front and back yards were spacious, and alongside the house ran a beautiful creek. Above the creek was a wooden bridge that made a lot of noise when cars went over it. We loved it all!

We also loved our neighbors. In fact, we keep up with some of them still today. Living in a small town was a joy. People often knew one another, and the kids could walk to school and play freely without a lot of worry on our part about their safety.

MARCIA COMMITS HER LIFE TO JESUS

When Marcia was eight, we were temporarily living in the repurposed, old store building. The Holy Spirit was talking to Marcia about committing her life to Christ. We told her, "Marcia, you can commit your life to Christ right now, right here. You don't have to be in church to be saved." Marcia prayed and trusted Christ alone for her salvation right there. I guess it was more than the old store that found new purpose!

A HEART FOR MISSIONS

We had great missionary programs for the children. We got the church kids excited about a two-month project to raise money to purchase a jeep for mission use in a foreign country. Each child saved their pennies in a jar at home. Sunday came and Marcia and Dwight each took a full jar of saved pennies to church. When they took the missionary offering for the jeep, Marcia dumped all of her coins in. Dwight, however, took only a little out of his jar to place in the offering.

Noticing this, Dave and I decided to use it as a learning opportunity for our kids. After church, we found coins at the parsonage and secretly filled Marcia's offering jar to the top with money.

Dwight got curious. "Marcia, you put all your money in the offering this morning. Why do you have a lot of money and I don't?" he inquired. "You put all your money in. I didn't. I should have more!"

Dwight having took the bait, I jumped into the conversation. "Oh, my word, what happened?" I said. "Look! Marcia has more money than she put in the missionary offering. Isn't that amazing?! I guess we should always remember that God will take care of us."

I think the lesson stuck. Dwight, Marcia, and David are all givers today. That pleases me. God loves good and cheerful givers!

OLD DRAPES, CHORE CHARTS, AND DANIEL BOONE

Someone had given us some old, heavy, brown-colored drapes, and I saved them for later use. The time came when I knew what to do with them. I was trying to teach the kids good hygiene, so I hung a chart in the bathroom for the kids to check off when they brushed their teeth, washed their face, made their bed, picked up their dirty clothes, etc. When they collected so many checks, I started to make that child a jacket—a Daniel Boone jacket! With every check, I would sew and create a little more—maybe attach the sleeve or stitch a pocket or even fasten a button. They loved those jackets! Their friends began asking if I could make them one too. And all the jackets cost me was the price of thread!

MUSICAL INSTRUMENTS TO PLAY AND SHARE

We bought Marcia a trumpet to play, and she got real good at it. Dwight wanted an accordion, so we found him one. David loved drums, so we bought a starter set for him. Music was always such an important part of Dave's life and mine; we're glad our kids gravitated toward it too. God really used music throughout the years to draw us and others closer to Him.

One day, a missionary came to visit who really needed an instrument. So, Dwight sold his accordion to him for a more than fair price so that the missionary could use it for ministry on the mission field. This wouldn't be the last time such a thing happened, but it began an important pattern of giving for Dwight to offer to the Lord whatever He might want or need for His plans and purposes.

DEATH OF DAVE'S DAD

Amid all the joy of our days in Sandy Lake, Dave's dad was battling cancer. His body eventually gave way, and he went to be with Jesus. Needless to say, it was a very sad day for our whole family when Dave's father died. We were so thankful for his example in our family's life and for setting the standards high in the ministry of the gospel.

DWIGHT'S HEARING LOSS AND HEALING

Dwight was born partially deaf. We didn't know he was deaf, so we just thought he didn't want to listen. I would try to call him for supper, and he wouldn't show up. At first, I thought he was just disobedient.

Then other clues to a hearing deficiency began showing up. Dwight would lay with his ear right next to the radio with the volume blaring. He wasn't selected in Christmas programs because no one could understand what he was saying. Equally, he learned to read lips to understand what others were saying, since he couldn't hear their words.

"Dwight is not hearing," I told the school principal. "In his class, please let him sit in the front row so he can lip-read."

"We can't keep him here at this school," the principal said. "He's in the second grade. We don't have what's needed to accommodate his learning with a hearing deficiency. He needs to attend the deaf boarding school in Erie, Pennsylvania."

Needing more help, we took him to our family physician. Among other questions, he asked, "Has Dwight ever had a runny nose?"

"No, come to think of it," I said.

"Dwight needs surgery," concluded the doctor. "I think his eustachian tubes are blocked."

The doctor continued, "Before we do surgery, however, I'd like to try one more thing. I am going to give him a special shot. After the first shot, do you have a nurse in your church who could give him a shot every week for a month? I will give you a supply."

"Yes, I do. Thank you," I replied.

Dwight could hear a little better after the doctor worked on him that day.

"God is going to heal our son," said Dave.

Dwight never had to have the surgery. The shots helped him. We prayed many prayers for his healing. Soon after, Dwight could hear as well as anyone.

While Dwight's hearing improved, his speech did not.

"Marcia, what did Dwight just say?" I found myself constantly saying. Marcia seemed to understand his words in a way we could not and did a lot of interpreting for us.

The school hired a speech therapist for Dwight to improve his vocabulary, but other children made fun of him. Kids laughed at him when they saw him in the school hallway with the speech therapist. So, Marcia volunteered to help Dwight at home.

"I'll help him with his sight words at home. He doesn't need those kids teasing him," Marcia said.

We thank God for God's healing and help through many vessels. No one who hears Dwight sing or speak publicly as an international evangelist would ever know he ever had a problem with his hearing or speech. God healed him just as Dave said and we believed. And we give God all the glory!

LESSON LEARNED, NO SPANKING

We told the kids they would get a spanking from us if they ever got one at school. One day, David came home and said the teacher spanked him to make him an example. None of the kids had done their homework. The teacher said that the next one who had not done their homework would get a spanking. The next one was David!

I called her that night, and she said, "Please don't spank him... I was wrong!" Needless to say, we did not give him a spanking. Some years later, that teacher gave her heart to Jesus at the church parsonage!

MISSIONARY STORIES, BLIND BOYS, AND BIKES

I told our kids missionary stories before they went to bed. One time I told the story of a little boy who was blind but wanted to do everything other kids did.

The next morning, little seven-year old David wondered what it would be like to be blind. He rode his bike with his eyes closed, ran into the creek, and cut his chin. I drove David to the doctor ten miles away while Marcia applied pressure on the wound with a towel. David got 10 stitches.

CAMP MEETINGS

Camp meetings are a treasured part of our spiritual heritage. The tradition goes back to the early days on the American frontier when people would gather once a year at the church campground, usually out in the country, for a week or more of special meetings.

Families from all over the countryside would gather to camp, worship, eat, pray, and seek the Lord. The meetings were often accompanied by powerful preaching, enthusiastic singing, and a spirit of revival.

Our family was often asked to do the special music and lead the singing for camp meetings and Bible conferences. At one camp meeting, when the children were singing a special musical number, a man in the congregation felt deep spiritual reverberations. He ran around the entire perimeter of wooden pews inside the tabernacle, shouting and waving his white hankie. On his second lap, he started down the center aisle. It was blocked by a wheelchair, so he started wildly jumping over the pews all the way to the back.

Our children were very surprised and shocked, but they kept singing!

STONEBORO LAKE

Up to the road was another small town, Stoneboro. It had a nice lake and a great swimming pool area. On hot days, I would take the kids up and leave them for several hours. They loved the water!

When David was about five or six, he would often climb up the high dive and jump. It scared the lifeguards to death. David became a great swimmer, and even became a lifeguard when he got older.

GREAT CHURCH, GREATHOUSE, GREAT FRIENDS

As for the Sandy Lake Wesleyan Church and God's blessing on this place—we loved these people from the very first. Among them were Gene and Lois Greathouse, relationships we made at Stoneboro Camp. We became dear friends through the years. Gene passed on, and Lois and I still keep in touch today.

CANTATAS, REVIVALS, AND OUTREACH

There were a lot of people at the Sandy Lake church who had great voices but rarely used them. Dave and I wanted to change that. We started a choir, formed quartets, and even coached and encouraged some people to sing solos. I played the piano and Dave directed.

God began to use music to minister to the people. We started Christmas cantatas. One of the first ones was "Born a King," a favorite of many.

The music ministry spurred on lots of other ministry. We had several revivals that were a weeklong. God really moved. We began to reach out to the town, and they began noticing that the Sandy Lake Church was open and welcoming to all.

CHRISTY CRITTER... THE ONE WHO LOVES JESUS

One time at a little league baseball game, Dwight saw one of the boys who had been bullying a lot of the kids at school and in the neighborhood. The boy didn't like something David did and went after him. Seeing this, Dwight chased after the bully. When he caught him, Dwight gave the kid a bloody nose. The boy ran home crying, and that was the end of bullying from the boy all the kids were afraid of.

That boy, years later, gave his life to Jesus! And now, he's still living a Christian life—married with children and grandchildren of his own. In fact, he's one of my Facebook friends. We call him "Christy Critter... the one who loves Jesus!"

BIKE RIDES AND DEVILISH DISGUISES

David took Bible stories literally. He was also very curious.

"Let's keep Sunday, the Sabbath Day, for holy things. No parks or bike riding," I said.

The next Sunday after dinner, while I was washing dishes, I saw David riding his bike.

"Why aren't you taking a nap? What are you doing out there riding your bike on Sunday?" I yelled through the kitchen door.

"Don't worry, Mom," David replied, "the devil will never know it's me, because I'm wearing Dwight's coat!"

WORSHIP, LOVE, AND COURTROOM MIRACLES

During our time at Sandy Lake, we saw true miracles of God. One miracle occurred in a courtroom of all places.

Let me begin by saying we often enjoyed sweet times of prayer and singing *after* our Sunday evening services. It was common in those days for people to bring their guitars to church with them. It was often after the formal service concluded that the real worship began. Someone would just go up to the piano and start playing. Those who loved music would stay, while everyone else filed out. It didn't take long before those gathered felt a little bit of heaven descend on us as we sang.

Learning to pray and worship our heavenly Father on Sunday prepared us for whatever came our way Monday through Saturday.

We needed that inspiration and preparation too, in the case of a man named Dan. Dan had married a woman who had a small boy from a previous marriage. Sadly, the small boy was afflicted with a strange disease that made his bones unusually brittle and liable to fracturing or breaking.

One day, this precious, little four-year old boy was walking with Dan in their barn when suddenly he stumbled. To a normal, healthy, young boy that would mean little more than a scrape on the arm or a bruised knee. Instead, to the shock and horror of Dan, the boy closed his eyes and never opened them again.

Of course, his parents called the ambulance and the police at once. When first responders arrived at the scene and tried to revive the young boy, they discovered he had multiple fractures. Their logical but unproven conclusion was that the boy had been abused. They accused Dan of beating the boy to death. They slapped handcuffs on Dan as he stood speechless at the unfounded accusation. The police loaded Dan into the back seat of the cruiser and took him to the county jail for arraignment on first degree murder charges.

If you're wondering what in the world these tragic events of Dan and his family have to do with a small country church that stays behind on Sunday evening to sing, pray, and worship, hang in there, there's more...

Word of Dan's arrest soon spread throughout our small community like wildfire. Now, if you've never lived in a small rural community like ours, this might be hard to understand. But country folk often have a natural instinct for knowing who is a bad sort and who is a good person. In this case, we all knew Dan could never have beaten his little son to death. We knew Dan, his wife, and their boy were a loving and caring family. There wasn't a single person in the entire community who believed Dan was guilty, except the police.

The entire church chose to stand behind Dan and his family. The day he appeared before the local magistrate on murder charges, the courtroom was filled to capacity by the time court was called to order. County folk far and wide came to show their support for Dan and his wife.

The scene was amazing. Farmers, gas stations workers, teachers, nurses, and housewives were all quietly standing in the courtroom in silent support of Dan. Many had their heads bowed and eyes closed in fervent prayer as they appealed to the True Judge of all the earth to intervene on Dan's behalf.

At the time, Dan was not a believer. Yet, as he turned his head and saw all his neighbors and church people crowded shoulder to shoulder on his behalf, tears formed in his eyes. He saw all the prayers being offered up on his behalf. The same spirit of prayer that prevailed on Sunday evenings after church was at work in the courtroom.

As the hearing began, the judge looked around the room and said, "What are all these people doing here?"

A man from our church stepped forward and said, "Your Honor, we are a neighborhood, a church, and a community who believes Dan didn't do this."

There was a long silence as the judge surveyed the unusual scene before him. He turned his gaze toward Dan seated at the defendant's table. The judge addressed Dan directly. "I want you to stand up for what I'm going to say."

Dan stood to his feet and swallowed hard. Those of us praying in the back of the courtroom squeezed one another's hands and prayed even more fervently for God to intervene.

What the Judge said next shocked us all. "You have too many people behind you to be guilty," the judge declared. "I don't believe you did it either. Case dismissed!"

An audible gasp could be heard throughout the courtroom. Smiles, handshakes, hugs, and tears filled the room.

As a result of God's miraculous answer to prayer that day at the Mercer County Courthouse, Dan and his wife committed their lives to Christ.

Their other son went on to become a doctor and serve as a medical missionary along with his wife in Africa. During the many decades they served, they often recalled the story how God miraculously delivered his father. Just a few years ago, Dan's son and his wife returned from the mission field in Africa to do medical missions work with Native American tribes in the Western United States.

* * *

TEN-FINGER PRAYER PAUSE: PRAYER AND ACTION

To pray requires a willingness and obedience to act. Prayer is so much more than asking God to fix, solve, remove, fulfill, or mitigate things. When we pray, we have a better understanding of what God is up to in our lives, in the lives of others, and in His Kingdom.

In Dan's story above, our collective time of worship and prayer on Sunday nights was so much more than for our own benefit. Make no mistake, it did benefit us—immensely! But it also prepared us to see what God was doing in Dan's life and provided the perspective and power to to participate with God in not only Dan's life, but his wife's life, his other son's life and the multiplied lives and decisions their lives interacted with and influenced for the sake of the Kingdom.

If you're serious about prayer, make sure your shoes are laced up tight at the end of your conversation with God. More times than not God will want to use you in the things you're praying about and the people you're praying for.

* * *

ONE FOOT ON EARTH, THE OTHER IN HEAVEN

God had called us to the ministry. So, wherever God would lead, we would go. That often meant moving frequently, living in less than plush homes, and having to depend on God's faithfulness to keep food on our table and gas in our car. Yet, it was a wonderful life as we experienced God's goodness, faithfulness, and love for us as a family over and again. I would not trade the life we lived for all of the gold and silver this life has to offer. I would much rather be in the service of the King.

We came to believe that serving the Lord in ministry is to have one foot on earth and one foot in heaven.

DISCOVERING THE "WHY" OF MY LIFE: PRAYER

The great American author, Mark Twain, though himself hardly a believer, once said something that rings true for followers of Christ:

 The two most important days of our lives are the day we are born. The second is the day we discover why.

As a child, during the sad years in the orphanage where I experienced deprivation, cruelty, and loneliness, I sometimes wondered if God put some people on earth just to suffer. It was a tough thing to wrestle with, given the circumstances of my childhood. It led to a second wondering: why was I born?

After high school, when I accepted Jesus as my Savior, I discovered the answer to the "why" question. I was born to serve Jesus with all my heart, soul, mind, and strength. As time went by, I began to discover with greater clarity what that meant in practical terms for my life. For me, it was my calling. I was to serve alongside my beloved husband, Dave, as a pastor's wife in the local church.

That calling became even more refined, defined, and clarified as the years went by, and my relationship with Jesus matured and deepened. As clear as an astronomer's telescope that peers into the starlit sky and brings far-off stars and galaxies into sharp focus, my Kingdom contribution and labor of love became easy to see. My unique calling was *prayer*. I was to engage an ongoing life of prayer for my loved ones, my church family, my neighbors, for friends not yet made, for strangers I would never meet, and for God's Kingdom to come. Prayer came in sweeping waves for revival and being burdened for the world. Prayer also came in the form of lifting to God the heart-cries and everyday needs of those around me on a daily basis.

PAST PAIN LEADS TO PRESENT INTERCESSIONS

Now, every believer should be a person of prayer. In fact, the Bible instructs us "to pray at all times…" (1 Thessalonians 5:17). But our Lord calls some people to a unique ministry of prayer, what some would call *an intercessor*. Intercessors are those who bring the needs and requests of others before the Lord in an intensive, prolonged and often passionate manner of prayer. This was the type of prayer calling God had for me.

God chose to use the heartbreaking events of my early childhood to help me understand the sorrows and pain other people experience. Somewhere, somehow, I learned to hear His voice when He told me it was time to pray for others who were suffering. My prayers of intercession sometimes came with instructions to give others a specific message God had for them. Other times, God directed me to respond with loving action.

8

LAKEVIEW

CALLING AND MOVE TO LAKEVIEW CHURCH

In 1969, we accepted a call to Lakeview Wesleyan Church in Marion, Indiana. We packed up our belongings, our three children, and journeyed to the familiar college town where two decades prior Dave graduated college and we lived as newlyweds.

When we arrived, we unloaded the truck, set the boxes in the parsonage, and headed straight out the door to... South Carolina! Yes, South Carolina. We had made a commitment to lead music for a church camp some time back and felt like we needed to follow through with the event. All went well at the church camp, and we returned to Marion. Finally, we got the chance to unpack everything and set up "home." Who knew that to move from Pennsylvania to Indiana one sometimes has to go through South Carolina!

After nine years of wonderful ministry in Sandy Lake, I naturally missed the people, the church, and the town. Dave said it was important not to go back and visit unless we were invited. He felt like the new pastor needed time and space to connect with people without needless comparisons or biases.

Lakeview was a great church and growing. It was one where we felt such a spirit of freedom, such a joyful expectation of the Lord's presence.

One of my first good memories was the fellowship we enjoyed after prayer meeting and choir practice. We would often go to Jerry's Restaurant on the bypass for something to eat and share conversations about family, community happenings, and the ins and outs of daily life.

UNCLE RED AND WANDA

Dave's best friend from college (and the men's quartet he and Dave were a part of) was Roland Conley. We kept up with Roland and his wife and would visit back and forth. We loved to reminisce about the college trips with our music team. The stories kept getting bigger and better whenever I would tell them. Dave and Red stuck closer to the facts. We referred to him so often as "Uncle Red" around our home, the kids came to believe he was their real uncle. We all loved to visit with Red and Wanda, and they felt the same about us. Yet, Red and Wanda were not believers. Our family prayed for Red and Wanda's salvation almost every night.

We often invited Red and Wanda to services at Lakeview Church. While Red was kind about it, he never attended. Wanda, however, began attending. In time, God answered our prayers for Wanda, and she got saved. We certainly rejoiced in that! But we were not about to give up until our dear friend Red came to know Jesus as Lord and Savior too!

APPLE PIES AND HOME ECONOMICS

Someone had given me a lot of apples, so I made eight apple pies. They smelled so good. Before supper, I had to go to the store for something, and while there I saw the high school home economics teacher. She was a newlywed, and her in-laws were to be at her home for dinner that evening. She shared how she had nothing home-baked for dessert. So, I told her to stop at my house and get two pies. After all, I had eight! She was excited, and I was happy I could help.

When I told Dave what I had done, he couldn't believe I gave her two pies. "She teaches baking at the high school!" he exclaimed.

That night, we had company over for our evening meal. When I served the pie and ice cream, I skipped over Dave. I told them he didn't want any. He couldn't believe I said that because he loves apple pie!

CUL-DE-SAC KIDS, SATURDAY MORNINGS, AND JOY!

We lived on a cul-de-sac in Marion, and I decided to reach out to the neighborhood kids. To my knowledge, none of the neighborhood kids attended any church or kids' club. There were a dozen homes and lots of kids.

In the 1960s and 70s, it was typical for kids to play outside and hang out on the streets from morning to evening, especially during summer breaks and after school. The kids rode their bikes everywhere. Outside of lunch and supper, the kids were out and about all day. Parents didn't worry as much about letting their children roam the neighborhood or have dinner at a friend's house.

With so much time and opportunity, the neighborhood kids became my mission field. On Saturday mornings, they couldn't wait to come to our house. I would put a bowl out containing folded up notes of what I needed done around the house. The notes included such chores as: clean the breakfast table, dust the front room, shake the rugs, put dishes in dishwasher, etc. To motivate the kids further, I'd place nickels and dimes around to remind them they were really getting paid!

Beyond needed house tasks, I made sure to include some fun assignments in the bowl too—things like, "Get on your bike, go around the block, and sing 'Jesus Loves Me!'"

At the end of the morning, the kids would bring all their notes to me, we'd check off their assignments, and then we all went to Dairy Queen for ice cream! They loved that!

Parents began wondering why the kids always wanted to go to the Robertson's on Saturday morning! I guess fun, love, earnings, and ice cream are wonderful motivators!

One summer day, I drove up to our home at the church dressed in some old work clothes. When I saw the kids playing ball in our backyard, I parked up the street. I shuffled down toward our backyard with my farmer bib overalls and old straw hat over my forehead.

"What do you think you're doing playing ball over here? You won't get away with anything!" I said, gruffly.

Thinking I was a no-gooder bothering and scaring the children, one of the boys, Robbie Pugh, ran over and tackled me to the ground. When they finally figured out it was me, we all had a good laugh. I was sore for days! You can bet I didn't play that trick again.

CLOSE NEIGHBORHOOD, SPRAWLED OUT SCHOOLS

The neighborhood had several kids that were the same age as our kids. Many of our neighbors had swimming pools too—that made it nice for the kids and easy to meet other children. The Pettis's had a boy about Marcia's age and a girl the age of one of our boys. Next door to us were the Clements. They had a boy about the age of Dwight. Another family had several girls. We soon discovered that most of the kids and their families didn't have a church home. We wanted to help change that.

A lot of the kids began coming to our house in the morning to catch the school bus. We were in the Gas City school district, and our kids all went to different schools: Mississinewa for Marcia, J.C. Night for Dwight, and Westview for David. Most of the church kids were in Marion's school district, so our kids hardly knew anyone when they began attending their new schools. They all felt a little lost at first.

FINDING GINGER AND A SAFE WAY HOME

While at Lakeview, we bought David a horse, Ginger, and boarded her close by. David loved Ginger. One day, Ginger got lost, and we went all around the area asking if anyone had seen her. We couldn't find her anywhere.

About a week later, Dave, David, and I went out again to find her. We took David out of school. As we walked around we heard a noise in the lowlands, and David ran down and hollered for Ginger. Sure enough, it was her. We found her. We went out to eat to celebrate. David was sure happy! Finding lost things and celebrating is a specialty of God's. I think finding Ginger helped us to remember that truth once again.

EVERYDAY LIFE, OUT-OF-THIS-WORLD LOVE

One family had a father who was the head of the local Coca-Cola plant. Tragically, his wife left him with six children to raise. With great intention, we consistently reached out to the family and invited the children to church. They responded. They heard the gospel, and Jesus brought healing to their hurting hearts. Years later, one daughter shared with me that had it not been for our personal invitations to church, she would have never come to know Jesus Christ as Lord. That woman, Carol, now serves on Forge's Board of Directors. *Dear ones, never underestimate the power of an invitation!*

In many ways, I was running a children's backyard Bible school—only it was year-round and permanent. It seemed to spread out in concentric circles as parents saw their children changing in Christ-filled ways. From our neighborhood, the Pettits's began attending Lakeview Church and eventually they were saved. Robbie Pugh, another neighbor, is now a minister. Carol, who I just mentioned, now has a daughter in full-time ministry. Just as I prayed for Carol, I now pray for her daughter and encourage her in her ministry.

A SPECIAL HEART FOR CHILDREN

I believe it was because of the loneliness, desperation, and hopelessness I experienced in my own childhood, that our Lord gave me a special love for children. I saw in the face of each child a reflection of my own experience, and I knew they needed to know the love of Jesus I had desperately desired as an undervalued, overlooked, and unloved orphan.

It thrills me today to be in contact with so many of the children I prayed for who eventually came to personally know Jesus. Children often shared their hurts, burdens, and hopes with me, and together we would seek the Lord in prayer. It was so good to rejoice with them, then and now, as God answered their prayers.

Along with serving at the church, I also worked full-time at the Wesleyan Church World Headquarters, located then, in Marion. Things were quite busy with my job, serving at the church, caring for our home, giving needed attention to our three children, and managing on my own while Dave was away on church business. Yes, I had my hands full, but it was one of the best times of spiritual growth in my life. I loved how it made my spirit soar!

CHILDREN'S CHURCH, HERBIE, AND SUNDAY DINNER

Our church was growing, and we started a children's church. I was in charge of ministry to our younger congregation while Dave preached in "big church."

I had a great helper with the children. His name was "Herbie." Herbie was a huge, stuffed monkey friend that Dave's uncle had given me. He stood about four feet tall and had a missing ear. I would talk to Herbie and led the children to believe that Herbie was talking to me. I wasn't a polished ventriloquist, but the kids thought Herbie was real. They all wanted to take Herbie home with them.

I had a basket to put boys names in and one for girls. Every Sunday the children would reach in and draw a name to see if it was their turn to eat Sunday dinner with my family. If their name was picked, they also got to choose the menu. It was often hamburgers and french fries.

I still hear from some of those kids today. It's amazing what a little meal and a lot of love can do.

THE GO CART THAT WOULDN'T STOP GOING

Someone gave David a go cart that had a little motor. Late one day he and a friend were out playing with it, and David's foot got caught underneath. It scraped David's foot raw. They rushed him into the emergency room. David said it was the worst pain he had ever had.

They shot needles into his foot with antibiotics to guard against infection. It was a sore sight to see, and it took a long time to heal.

REVIVAL FIRE AND SPIRITUAL AWAKENING

During our time at Lakeview, our church and family witnessed and experienced a true spiritual awakening. It began at Asbury College in Wilmore, Kentucky, in a normal weekday chapel service that unexpectedly ran late.

The college had chapel every morning for the students. At the beginning of a chapel service one ordinary campus day, a girl from the back walked down the side aisle of the chapel and made her way to the platform and stopped at the mic facing the assembly of students, faculty, and staff.

Though shy, she began to speak. The room fell silent as she began to share her story. Hearts and heads were attentive. She began saying that God was speaking to her, and she wanted to give her testimony. The Holy Spirit was palpable in that place. Before long, others lined up and began sharing their story. The chapel was filled with the presence of God.

The students stayed in the chapel and never got to their next class. Students shared honestly, and openly confessed their sins, sought reconciliation with one another, and trusted Christ for their salvation.

The teachers didn't understand why their students weren't showing up for class. Once they got word, many of them came over to the chapel to witness it for themselves. Seeing what God was doing, the administration canceled classes for the day.

No one could have foreseen those services would last nearly seven days without interruption. Students went home and began sharing all that had happened and all that God continued to do. The result was a spark of revival that burst into a full-fledged spiritual fire of renewal and awakening.

The campus-wide revival at Asbury sparked a movement that sent students out on the weekends all over America to share God's revival fire. Students traveled from Kentucky to Indiana to give their testimonies how God had become more real to them than they could have ever imagined.

Next thing we knew, news about the revival was in the newspaper in Anderson, Indiana, a city about 30 miles from where we lived. "Revival" headlined the paper for several days. One of the articles mentioned that the courthouse was open for prayer in the courtroom during the lunch hour, and that people could come and see what was happening if they so desired. When I read that, I wanted to go. I wanted to see what God was up to! As we traveled to Anderson, I remember praying, "Lord, I want the real thing! I want the fire of *Your* love. Please don't let this be just a flash fire!"

We got to the courthouse a few minutes early, and the lady at the front desk said the courtroom was on the second floor. Upon our arrival, the room was empty. So, we took a seat on the fifth or sixth row and waited for whatever was next.

In just a few minutes, the room was full of people bringing their lunches and filled with expectation. There was no formal beginning, and no particular person who seemed to be in charge.

Like a spark on seasoned kindling, the Holy Spirit lit a spiritual fire in that place. People spontaneously began singing praise to God. At the end of a song or hymn, someone would give their testimony. Then, more praise and prayer followed by someone else sharing. There was a wonderful feeling of God's presence that filled the room.

About two seats from me, a man stood up and said,

 You all know me as the town drunk. I can't read to get a job, and I walk the street and drink. Some kid came up to me and shared about this man, Jesus. Then, the kid prayed for me! Something happened, and now all I can tell ya is I'm a new person!

The man then asked someone near him if he could see their Bible a second. The man who couldn't read began reading from the Bible. He said, "I still can't read a newspaper, but I can read this Bible!"

As he read there right beside me, my heart leapt for joy! God was so real!

After the gathering ended and we were leaving the courtroom, we saw some teenagers standing in the back who had just walked in. They looked curious as to what had just happened there. We gladly shared what God had done and what He was doing. We told them we were from Marion and that we were having a youth rally on Sunday afternoon at our church and they were invited. When God is moving and people are responding, you just want to tell as many people as you can!

Soon, the fire of spiritual renewal reached our town too. Spiritual sparks spread into engulfing revival flames. It was so real, so supernatural, so unforced and unrehearsed. We prayed and prayed, and then prayed some more... until the glory of God fell on our congregation for the next 10 days.

"There is more, Agnes. There is more," I sensed God saying to me. I was listening and ready to respond. Whatever God asked, I was going to do.

Sunday came and the church was packed with youth and college kids. All of a sudden, we saw the teenagers from the courthouse in Anderson upfront and getting ready to share. It was amazing! God was powerfully present. Young and old started coming to the altar to meet with God. Some students from Marion College left the service to get their friends and bring them back. God was lighting the heart and lives of our youth and young adults on fire!

The college kids missed their evening meal. Someone suggested that maybe we would have extra food next door at the parsonage. Before we knew what was happening, scores of young people were over, and soon our refrigerator and cupboards were bare. We didn't care. We were so happy that God was at work and we had something for them to eat.

After the first day of revival that Sunday, Dave assured the congregation he would open the church Monday night if he saw cars pulling into the parking lot after dinner. Monday evening came, and sure enough, the parking lot was jammed packed. People couldn't get enough of God. They lined the altar and prayed for heaven to shower God's blessings and power on our church.

THE HOLY SPIRIT WAS OUR EVANGELIST

A Methodist pastor from Pennsylvania called and asked what was going on. I said our church was in revival. He asked about the preacher, and I said, "There is no preacher, only God and His presence." The preacher responded, "I need this. I'm coming!" He did, and he went home with fire in his heart. Revival soon started in his church too!

For ten evenings, the Spirit of God poured down on our church and community. I was experiencing fresh spiritual vitality and God led me away from my legalistic tendencies and upbringing. I was a doer-doer-doer, but I realized through the revival, Jesus had *done* it all already. All I needed to do was to encounter, enjoy, and respond to His love, joy, and grace.

It's a simple thing, really, but for the first time in my life, I freely wore my wedding ring, which before fellow Christians had frowned upon. God used the revival to help me set aside religious things for relational depth with Him and others. It was a first "taste" of the kind of life and freedom a fresh experience with God can bring.

LAKEVIEW HOME BIBLE STUDY

One Sunday morning, I was singing in the choir and saw a young couple come into worship. The choir member sitting next to me leaned over and whispered with excitement, "That's my boss!" The boss was a very wealthy man, but apparently money wasn't enough to satisfy him in life. He and his wife had young sons, and they felt it important that their family find a church. The husband's aunt happened to live across from the church. One day, he stopped and asked her about a church to go to and she suggested he and his family try ours. They came and found out it was just what they needed.

Soon, the husband and wife asked us to start a Bible study in their home. They said if we would lead it, they would get people there. And they did!

People came for all kinds of reasons to the Bible study. Many were spiritual hungry. Some were there, truthfully, just because they wanted to see the family's gorgeous house! So, the husband and wife gladly gave them a tour and then invited them to join us. We were amazed at how spiritually hungry people were to study God's Word and grow deeper in their relationship with Jesus.

GOING FISHING AT THE COUNTRY CLUB

Sometime later, another affluent couple in town began attending our services. He and his wife began inviting and bringing couples from the Marion Country Club to church. Dave and I led a Bible study in their home, and the country club soon started to hear a lot about Jesus. Many of these people were powerfully saved and have walked with Jesus for a lifetime!

One day, my friend, Mrs. Bell, called me to say she would be by to pick me up. "We're going fishing," she said. At first, I thought I should put on my fishing clothes. Then I realized she was inviting me to lunch at the country club. To her, fishing was not casting a line with a minnow and bobber; it was meeting women on the patio at the club house and telling our personal stories about how Jesus changed our life. Praise God, "fishing" was quite good at the country club!

HOLY LAND, HOLY PAPERS, HOLY HAPPENINGS

We had some great times at Lakeview those four years. I remember the church wanted Dave to go to the Holy Land, and they raised money for him to go. So many donations came in that they wanted me to go too. I was so excited. But I also realized I had no birth certificate. All I had was an adoption certificate. But even that wasn't in my possession, and we didn't have time for my folks to find it and get it to me.

Our pursuit of a birth certificate took Dave and I to Chicago. We filled out papers as best we knew how, and they said, "We'll get back to you." It was Thursday, and we were to leave the following Tuesday. Short of a miracle, it looked like I would not be going to the Holy Land with Dave.

Sunday came and Dave was preaching. During the worship service, a man came into the church and asked to see the pastor. An usher told the man that the pastor was preaching, but that his wife was sitting in the backseat. The man came to where I was sitting and handed me my needed travel papers!

I packed the next day, and, on the following one, Dave and I were on the plane to the Holy Land. Dave's mom lived with us, so we had someone to watch the kids and house while we were gone. My folks also traveled from Michigan to help. God provided every last detail.

Once in Israel, it was a wonderful experience to see the places Jesus walked and lived. One night, we walked in Old Jerusalem. It was cold and damp, and a man was watching us. He came up and asked if we were Christians. When we told him we were. He asked if we would like to go to church the next morning. When we said yes, he said he would be across the street in the morning. He said he would find us. "When you see me," he instructed, "don't come up to me, just follow me at a distance."

The next morning we saw him and followed him as he directed. We walked behind him a couple blocks. As we trailed behind him up a number of steps, there was the church!

Before the service, they asked if anyone played the piano. I raise my hand. I went from spectator to piano player! Three different languages were spoken there, so it took a while to sing each song. It was a long service, but meaningful. The preacher had to preach in three languages!

Back at the hotel, they said there was a lady who would wash my hair and put it up like I liked it. It didn't go as planned, and my hair was a mess. I just combed my hair out because we were leaving the next morning and had little time to do much more with it. When we got to the airport, security was on high alert. The airport had been terrorized during the night. It was a chaotic and disheveled scene.

Because of my long, dark hair and dark complexion, they took me to an interrogation room to question me while Dave waited outside. I had some foot lotion that was Avon. They tasted it, smelled it, even put some on the wall and called an examiner in to inspect it. The examiner saw really fast it was Avon and finally let me go to catch my flight with Dave.

All this happened on the tails of the Six-Day War in the Holy Land! We reported back to the church with pictures and stories of all we had seen and heard. What an experience!

9

RETURN TO SANDY LAKE

RETURN TO SANDY LAKE

We didn't want to move, but Dave felt our family life was suffering with the active pace Lakeview Church demanded. It was a heavy load for all of us, but especially for our son, David, who was in 5th grade. It was the early 1970s, and people wanted more outreach programs on behalf of the church. As a result, Dave was gone more nights than he was home.

As we weighed the decision to move, we had to examine our priorities as a family. Dave knew this meant we needed a less active environment. So, based on our values, not the size or success of church ministry, we chose to pursue a closer family life.

After four years at Lakeview, it was time to move on. We got a call from the Sandy Lake church to come back. Truthfully, I really didn't want to go, but we felt God saying "go," and for me, that settles the issue every time. I didn't tell Dave what I was feeling, because I didn't want my attitude to affect him. Regardless of how I felt at the time, the decision proved to be a right and good one. Dave said sometime later about our move, "Now I have more time for our marriage, children, and family."

We moved to Sandy Lake and brought David's horse with us. We pulled into town after dark, got a key, and went into the parsonage. We were tired and cold. Having nothing unpacked yet, we took down the heavy drapes and covered with them as we slept on the floor. Sleeping anywhere that night sounded wonderful—we didn't about the location or the comfort of the sleep surface.

The next morning, David found a place up the hill about a quarter-mile away that would board his horse. It was with an older couple, the Miller's. We unloaded our belongings once again into the parsonage, and Dave's mom got an apartment a few blocks away owned by the Vogan's.

Regardless how I felt about moving before we left Marion, I made up my mind I was going to do my part to honor what God had asked me to do. Life is full of adjustments, and I had many. Once again, God was helping me renew my focus and trust His plan and provision.

Marcia was excited to be coming back to Sandy Lake because she still had a lot of friends there. It was 1973, and she had just graduated from high school. Her post-grad plans included singing with a music group called "Celebrations." The ministry group traveled throughout the United States—singing in schools, churches, and wherever else they were invited.

Traveling with the Celebrations, Marcia received a scholarship to Marion College (now Indiana Wesleyan University). Dwight was taking his 11th and 12th grade high school years together because he also wanted to travel and sing with the group. That summer, Dwight also spent several weeks in Puerto Rico working at a Christian school. He turned 16 while he was there. Our kids were making the most of their young lives.

A GOOD POUNDING

At Sandy Lake, one of the sweetest things our church ever did was to give us "poundings." Now, it might seem somewhat harsh, even brutal, to do such a thing to the pastor and his wife, but "poundings" in Sandy Lake meant something unusually good and different than the way we often think of that word. To give someone a "pounding" meant everyone would bring a *pound* of food to give to the pastor and his family. It was a unique and dear expression of love. It also helped with the ongoing food needs of a growing family!

When I returned home from prayer meeting one Wednesday evening, our kitchen counter was full of food. The congregation had surprised us with another pounding, and not a moment too soon. We really needed the groceries. Not so much for our family, but to feed the many people who stopped by our home for a meal. There was beginning to be so many that we were starting to have trouble feeding them. Because we lived on a major state road, access to our home was easy, and people often came by—neighbors, strangers, and longtime friends just traveling through.

FISH AND LOAVES SUNDAY DINNER

One Sunday morning, we had a total of 32 people visit from our previous appointment at Lakeview Church. Grocery stores weren't open on Sundays in those days, and I didn't know where we could get enough food to feed them all. During Sunday worship at the church, I prayed silently for "fishes and loaves to be multiplied."

Some ladies in the church volunteered to help me put everything together for Sunday dinner. It wasn't a planned event either. In fact, no one knew that the other 32 from Marion were coming. And then, the gathering just kept on growing. One family showed up with six kids. A truck driver stopped and knocked at the door. I nearly had to look outside to see if a big billboard was in our yard with the invitation, "Genuine home cooking here, everyone welcome!"

As God always does, He supplied our need. God knew in advance who was driving through and when that Sunday. That's why God prompted the people the Wednesday night before to give us a "pounding." As someone once said, "God is never too early and never too late. He's always right on time!"

SANDY LAKE WOMEN AND THE PARSONAGE BASEMENT

God burdened my heart for the women in the community. I knew that meant reaching out to them in the daily routines and pressures of life. I wanted to come alongside them in practical ways to help with such things as giving them a listening ear about raising their children or getting stains out of their kids' overalls or helping find ways to stretch the family budget.

One of those community connections was inviting them to make crafts as Christmas presents for their friends and relatives. It started when I got together with my friends, Lois and Phyllis, to do a devotion and a craft. We had so much fun, we decided to do it again the following month and invite others to join us. The basement of the parsonage, spacious and new, seemed the perfect place to do such a thing.

Once a month women from the Sandy Lake community would come. We had them write their name on a name badge and wear it so we would know who they were.

At the end of our craft time, I would talk about Jesus and what did on the cross for each of us. Then, I would pray for Jesus to cleanse us from sin so we could each have a clean heart. I invited them to receive Jesus as their Lord and Savior if they had never done so.

"If you asked Jesus into your heart as we prayed," I'd instruct them, "put an 'X' on the back of your name tag and leave it on the table. We'd love to talk to you more about your decision." The first time we did that, six name tags had an "X" on the back!

It wasn't long before women were coming from just about every church in the area. They began offering their churches to host our gathering. We were honored, but we continued to meet in the parsonage basement. The women's gathering grew in leaps and bounds. Soon 40 were attending. Then, 55. And as we grew, so did the number of women putting an "X" on their name tag. By the time we left, we had as many as 183 women gathering in our parsonage basement for crafts, a message, and prayer!

THE PROMINENT PASTOR'S WIFE

During our gatherings, the pastor's wife of a prominent church in the area called me and said the women of their church really liked coming to the craft gathering and wondered if she could come too. "Yes! Of course you're welcome to come," I said.

When she came, I spoke once again about what it means to have a *personal* relationship with Jesus. After the gathering, I noticed she had placed an "X" on her name tag. I called her and she confirmed that indeed she had put the "X" on her badge. She knew *about* God for a lot of years, but she never knew about having an up-close, personal relationship *with* Jesus and His Spirit dwelling within us.

The next month, the pastor's wife came to the gathering again. She was so excited about what God was doing in her life! I called her that night. She shared with me how the last month had been a new and wonderful experience. She said she always loved singing in the choir, telling children Bible stories, and other things that went on in the church, but she was excited that Jesus was so real in her life. What a testimony she shared that night on our call!

The next morning, the phone rang and it was her husband, the reverend. He asked me, "Did you call my wife about 8 o'clock last night?"

I said "Yes, we had quite a talk!"

With great sadness in his voice, he said, "You were the last one to talk to her… last night, she died in her sleep."

We never know the importance of a single moment and opportunity that will impact a life for eternity.

CHRISTMAS MIRACLES MULTIPLIED

At the Sandy Lake parsonage, we had a buzzer on the phone that was connected to the church next door. That way, if Dave or I needed to get in touch with one another, we could simply push the buzzer. One day, a man visited the parsonage and asked to speak to the "Father." I knew he meant "pastor," so I buzzed Dave's office. Dave came over and the two went back to the church to talk further.

When Dave came home for lunch, he told me about their conversation. The man had six children and another one on the way. He and his wife were two months behind in house payments. They were in a tough spot.

I knew Dave had borrowed money from our insurance policy to help pay for our family's Christmas. I also knew he had just gotten the money in hand. Dave told me what I didn't want to hear. He gave our borrowed Christmas money to the man. Truthfully, I was mad. This was Christmas money for our kids! But, Dave's heartstrings were tugged, and he felt they really needed it. And now, we were left where we started, with no money for Christmas.

Soon after, a friend asked me to go shopping with her in a much larger town. Normally, I would have been thrilled to go, but since we had no money, I told her I couldn't make it. I didn't want to tell her the real reason—that I simply didn't have money to shop.

My friend was persistent. She asked me a second time and then a third. Tired of dodging the question of why I couldn't go, I told her I would make the trip. Dave gave me $10; he didn't want me to be empty handed for the day. "Hopefully," he said, "you can at least have a meal with her."

We stopped at a drugstore that served lunch. I saw balloons hanging from the ceiling, and the server said "Pick one. You might win a banana split!" I picked one, and sure enough, I only had to pay one cent for a large banana split. I had enough money for lunch and got a "cherry on top" as well.

We walked out of the drugstore and began shopping. It was a windy day, and on the sidewalk I found a $10 bill. I picked it up and begin looking around for someone who may have dropped it. The only one I saw was a man going into a nearby store. I ran to him to ask if it was his.

"Sir," I said, "Did you happen to lose some money just now?"

"Yes," he responded.

"How much?" I asked.

"Whatever you found!" he said as he laughed.

Knowing it wasn't his, I just added $10 to my Christmas money! It is hard to believe, but I got so many sales that day that when I got home, I had all I needed for Christmas. How great was that!

Years later, the man to whom Dave gave our Christmas money told Dave how he went on to help someone else in need at Christmas. Even better, the man's daughter later gave her heart to God. Talk about gifts that keep on giving!

GOD CHEERS AND CHEESEBURGERS

The Lakeview Church in Indiana was paying much more than Sandy Lake Church had the size and ability to match. The district superintendent came to the Sandy Lake Church board meeting one night and told them that they were compensating us much less than our former church provided.

After the meeting, the DS came to the parsonage to tell us we had gotten a big raise. We were so excited. It was late, but Dave told us to get our coats on because we were going to Sharon, a city about 5 miles away, to McDonald's to celebrate. What a night we had!

ANSWERED PRAYERS: UNCLE RED SAVED

The pastor who followed us at Lakeview Church, Dr. Gene Cockrell, invited us to return for a ministry visit to do the preaching and music for one of their annual revival meetings.

The first night, our three children sang several special numbers and then sat on the front row. When it came time for the altar call, Uncle Red, who lived in Marion and had come to the special service just to see us (He still hadn't been attending church in those days) was the first one down to the altar! After all these years, and many prayers, Uncle Red finally put his trust in Jesus Christ as his Savior! We had prayed as a family for him for two decades. The whole Robertson family went and kneeled beside him to pray. We thank God for answering our prayers for Uncle Red's salvation.

* * *

TEN-FINGER PRAYER PAUSE:
PRAYERS OF PRAISE AND
THANKSGIVING

Not all ten-finger prayers are one's with hands held high and begging for help. Quite the contrary. Sometimes, our hands are passionately held high out of sheer gratitude and praise for God's goodness, provision, and care.

You can be assured that our arms were extended to the heavens, our fingers outstretched, and our hearts were overflowing as we praised God for Red's salvation that glorious day. "Give thanks to the Lord, for He is good; His steadfast love endures forever" the psalm-writer tells us many times over in Psalm 136.

Our hands often found need to extend toward heaven and pray prayers of gratitude for what God had so lovingly and graciously done in our hearts, our lives, and in those of others. Whether a prayer lifted to give thanks for the beauty of the day, the joy on someone else's face, provision for daily needs, or the life-changing impact of one's salvation —God is worthy to be recognized, honored, and glorified for every good gift! "Give *thanks* in all circumstances," I Thessalonians 5:18 tells us. And that's what I intend to do as long as I have breath to do it. I hope you will too!

* * *

GOD'S CAN FIND YOU WHEREVER YOU ARE

One of the reasons I had previously thought we should stay at Lakeview Church was to foster Marcia, Dwight, and David's music interests. They were each growing professionally in their musical talents and gifts, and I thought that a bigger city would mean better opportunities for them musically. I was wrong. Bigger venues, cities, and opportunities aren't what God needs to employ someone for Kingdom service. God can find and use us wherever we are geographically—whether in well-known metropolitan areas or relatively unknown rural settings.

God was more than capable to launch our three kids, one by one, into music ministries from the small town of Sandy Lake, Pennsylvania. I shouldn't have been surprised. After all, Jesus got his start in an obscure little town to: Bethlehem.

10

PLYMOUTH

CALL TO PLYMOUTH WESLEYAN

After our second tenure at Sandy Lake, we were called to serve Plymouth Wesleyan Church in Plymouth, Indiana. God had reaffirmed to me in Sandy Lake that obedience is the best stride to have when walking with Him. Now, God was calling us to serve the people of Plymouth. We gladly said yes to God's bidding. Plymouth Wesleyan Church was familiar to Dave and me. We had been there for a revival years before. Dave would serve as pastor, and I would begin setting up "home." Builders were putting their finishing touches on a brand new parsonage next to the church. We would be the first to move into it. That made that part of the move both nice and exciting.

We were ready for any mission and challenge God had for us there. We heard the people in the church were friendly and loyal to one other, but the community saw them as isolated from the town. We were ready to love the congregation, love the Plymouth community, and share God's love and gospel message however, wherever, and whenever possible.

CLIFFORD THE CARPENTER HEALED

The scenery may have changed for us throughout the years, but the power of prayer remained steady and true wherever we called home. Plymouth was no exception. A couple named Clifford and Perma Guyer attended our church for a long time. One Sunday morning, when Dave asked for prayer requests, Clifford was the first to stand and speak:

 I have a personal prayer request to share. My whole adult life, I have worked as a carpenter to earn the income our family needs, but now I can't work because I haven't been able to lift my arms over my head. Please pray for my arms to be restored.

Dave invited Clifford forward so we could pray for him right then and there. "We'd like to anoint you with oil and pray for your healing in the strong and powerful name of Jesus, Clifford. Is that okay with you?" Dave asked.

Clifford agreed and was glad to receive the prayer. God answered our prayer, and we only had to wait a week! The next Sunday morning, Clifford was the first to his feet when Dave asked for prayer requests or praises:

 I am here today to testify to God's healing for my arms. I can lift them high over my head now. God has made it possible for me to provide a living for us as a carpenter. Praise the Lord!

Clifford waved his arms high several times above his head. The congregation who had been praying for him all week, clapped loudly and offered shouts of praise for God's gracious answer to our prayer.

MARCIA'S WEDDING

When Marcia was in college at Marion (Indiana), she met a fellow student, Garry Lauber. In time, they fell in love and decided to marry. The wedding was to take place at Lakeview Church in Marion.

On the day of the wedding, Marcia accidentally left all her going-away clothes in Plymouth (some 70 miles away). When Marcia realized what she had done, there wasn't enough time to go back and retrieve her clothes.

I told Marcia I would take care of it. I went to a store close to the church and explained what happened. They were so helpful. They helped me find the right clothes and sizes and had me back to the church in plenty of time for the wedding. Problem solved, and no one was the wiser. Marcia and Garry had a beautiful wedding.

PLYMOUTH PLUSES

David was in his senior year of high school where he lettered in tennis and sang for a number of special occasions, including a duet at his graduation.

Our first grandchild was born during our time there.

Two years into our assignment at Plymouth Wesleyan, Dwight came on staff as the youth pastor and music minister, and he lived in the old parsonage.

A doctor and his wife began attending our church and offered to let the youth meet in a new building he had built. It was great place for youth. The front of the building had a round pit with benches in it. The youth loved it.

Dwight joined the Optimist Club and became "Man of the Year."

DAVID AND JOHN DAVIDSON

While we were in Plymouth, David heard on TV that a popular singer and entertainer, John Davidson, was putting together a music camp on

Catalina island in California. David auditioned for the camp and made it!

While there, he met Tom. Tom was a piano player who could play anything. After the music camp was over, David and some other camp attenders stayed in California. He met a number of people there who are still his friends today.

A HORSE, A TRUCK, AN ANSWERED PRAYER

David had to move from Sandy Lake to Plymouth just before his senior year of high school. It's hard to try to make new friends so close to high school graduation.

David's horse, Ginger, needed to be transported from Sandy Lake to Plymouth. Given the tough timing of our move for David and his schooling, it was important that we find a way to get Ginger to Plymouth. He loved that horse more than anything in the world. When every attempt to get Ginger transported failed, the people of Plymouth Wesleyan made Ginger's transportation a matter of prayer.

Once again, God heard and answered our prayer. A man from another church in town had a semi-truck and heard about our need. "I'd be more than happy to bring Ginger to Plymouth on one of my trucking trips," he said. It wasn't long before he had a trip and picked up David's horse. There was great rejoicing when Ginger reunited with David.

MOPED MINISTRY

I had my realtor license, so it made it easy to connect with strangers. I noticed a little house where a lady lived who rode a moped everywhere. Dorothy Baird and I got aquatinted and eventually became friends. In time, she agreed to go to church and eventually got saved! She was cheerful and active in the ministry of the church and did a lot of work for God's Kingdom before she died. Who knew how much a moped, God's Kingdom, and a real estate license had in common!

DWIGHT, A GOOD DOCTOR, AND THE GREAT PHYSICIAN

While Dwight was attending Marion College, he became very ill. The doctors could not find what was wrong with him and sent him away to a clinic. With no answers there, they sent him home. We thought we might lose him. It was quite a scare.

Dr. Robert McIntyre had given Dave a book called, *God's Healing Community.* We began putting into practice the "triangle of care" the book taught: church elders anointing with oil, the medical community providing physical care, and the church body fervently praying.

We called for a healing service at church and anointed Dwight with oil. The church was praying and a young doctor, Byron Holm, came into our lives with fresh ideas how to treat Dwight through nutrition and specialized care.

In time, Dwight began to recover. He became stronger and regained a healthy appetite and countenance. While we participated with God through prayer, anointing, and medical care, there was never a doubt who did the healing: it was the Great Physician! Dwight was strong enough in a couple months to be hired on staff as the music and youth pastor for Dave!

This experience became a catalyst to a deep and lasting friendship with Dr. Holm and his family. They started coming to our church and became so much more than church attenders; they became lifelong friends and family members.

Marcia and Garry continue to live in Plymouth all these years (currently more than forty!) and have enjoyed a deep kinship with the Holm's. We love all the people at Plymouth Wesleyan and still try to visit as often as we can.

* * *

TEN-FINGER PRAYER PAUSE: HEALING PRAYERS

Here's what I know: God heals. Sometimes, God heals miraculously and instantly. Other times, God heals over a prolonged period of time and process. Still other times, God heals mysteriously and ultimately through hard to understand things, like death.

I know God heals. I know, because I've watched Him heal time and again throughout my life. He's healed bodies, relationships, emotions, communities, memories, churches, marriages, families, addictions, grieving hearts, wounded spirits, and sin-sick souls. He's healed me. He's healed those I know and love. He's healed people who were strangers to me. He's healed those who seemingly deserved it and those who seemingly did not. God is a God of life. And the God of life heals and restores.

That's why prayer is so important in the healing process. Prayer aligns our heart and mind with God's healing plan and purposes. It gives us opportunity to depend on, lean into, trust, find strength in, and be present with God in deeper ways. Prayer helps us to trust and love and act regardless of our hoped for outcomes and limited view of life and eternity.

God heals and prayer matters. One needs not understand it all to enter into it. Perhaps you can start here as you pray for healing; it's a passage of scripture that's meant so much to me over the years:

> *Praise the Lord, my soul;*
> *   all my inmost being, praise his holy name.*
> *Praise the Lord, my soul,*
> *   and forget not all his benefits—*
> *who forgives all your sins*
> *   and heals all your diseases,*
> *who redeems your life from the pit*

and crowns you with love and compassion,
who satisfies your desires with good things
so that your youth is renewed like the eagle's.

— PSALM 103:1-5

* * *

SOME TOUGH COOKIES

At times, people can be hard to love. I remember one or two girls at the Plymouth church who, for some reason, didn't like me at all. I remember putting Bible verses in my shoes when I would go over to the church to face them. Sometimes, I would tape a verse under my sleeve. God really helped me to keep my mouth shut and to love them as He did.

SHARING AT THE NURSING HOME

The opportunity came to start going to a nursing home to share and minister to the residents. When I would get to the home, I would go around to the various rooms and let the residents know we were about to begin. Some could make it to the meeting area on their own, others had to be wheeled up.

There was an old square piano in the meeting room. I would play and the residents would sing from song books I provided. A favorite request they liked to sing was "I'll Go Where You Want Me to Go, Dear Lord." Whenever we sang that song, I would get so tickled. All I could think about was how "going where God wanted them to go" would be hard since most of them needed help to get back to their room!

I didn't let Marcia know what I was doing, but I would go to her house and get her son, Jeremiah (who couldn't walk yet) and take him with me to the nursing home. The residents loved having him there. I would put Jeremiah on the lap of a resident while we sang one verse, then another resident would hold him on the next verse. They really look forward to seeing him and then holding him. I didn't tell Marcia until years later!

I loved ministering to the folks at the nursing home. Their smiles and joy were reward enough! While I in no way expected it, I was so honored when the governor of the state of Indiana, Otis Bowen, gave me an award for volunteering at the nursing home.

After the governor's passing, his wife, Carol, attended one of Forge's summer equipping events, *Deep Camp*, and began actively participating in the ministry. She also thought it fitting that Dwight have the electronic organ that the governor had. The organ now sits in Dwight's front room and is often played and enjoyed.

DELIVERY NURSE AND OTHER GOD ASSIGNMENTS

One never knows on any given day what his or her God-assignment might be. One day while living in Plymouth, my assignment was that of "Delivery Nurse." I had the experience of helping a doctor deliver a baby girl.

A pregnant woman came to our front door crying and not knowing what to do. Her husband had just left her, she had two or three other children, and was due with another child any moment. The expecting mother had only one relative, who lived in another state quite far away. I told her I would be there to help and so would our church.

I stayed by her side through her delivery and our church people helped with gifts, food, and needed supplies. It was Christmas time. What a joy to experience God's love for us in the birth and gift of Jesus in such a tangible way.

On another day, God assigned me the task of "Grief Counselor." I became friends with another girl who had just lost her dad and had no mother. We are still friends today. She lives in Washington State and I in Colorado, but we often call each other and pray together.

God had met me with His presence and power so many times during difficult times and seasons. What a joy and privilege to be present with others in the tough times and trials.

11

LAKEVIEW, PART TWO

MINISTRY BACK IN LAKEVIEW

After five years at Plymouth Wesleyan, our friend, Dr. Gene Cockrell, who was serving as senior pastor at Lakeview Wesleyan, asked Dave to return to Marion and join him in co-pastoring the church. Lakeview Church continued to flourish after our first tenure there and added a school and counseling center to its ministry. More pastoral leadership was needed, and Gene was asking us to come.

Sensing God's call to go, we bought a home in Marion. It was our first home that actually belonged to us and was not a church-owned and maintained parsonage.

I got my real estate license renewed, and I went to work for Century 21. I knew a lot of people in the area, so I did very well. One month, a company with which I had a great relationship was moving their company out of Marion. I listed 32 of their employees' homes and sold a good number of them. My listing and sales that month became a four-state convention record (Thank you, Lord!).

Dave and Gene worked and pastored well together.

Gene's wife and I co-chaired a women's group that met once a month on a weekday evening. It was a time for women to get together and share. New women were coming frequently and many of them began coming on Sundays as a result of their involvement in the women's group.

Our Sunday school class, which I had the privilege of teaching for a while, included about 100 people.

God blessed the church with wonderful musicians and people with beautiful singing voices. Sundays were filled with music. It was so inspiring. Many times the outpouring of God's presence would lead to pop-up testimonies.

LAKEVIEW YOUTH "MIRACLE CAMP"

Dwight was leading the youth at Lakeview Church. We couldn't get them to sign up for the Wesleyan youth camp, so we decided to start our own. We called it "Miracle Camp." Miracle Camp was located in Michigan. We had a good number of kids that came. I think it was an athletic club that owned it. There was a lake there and plenty of things for the youth to do during the day.

In the evening, we had services for the youth. A group of us who were leaders went to the gathering place early to pray over every seat. We knew those seats would soon hold a person God dearly loved and wanted to reach. God did a number of miracles.

Dwight invited a young boy, Mick Veach, to come to the camp. Mick committed his life to Jesus and received a miracle of his own. Mick now preaches for Forge, our ministry in Denver, Colorado.

Kerry Bowman and some of the Benson boys were there too. So many who attended had reason to believe in the miracles of God. Young people came back changed!

God moved in unexpected ways. Some of the girls gathered (in the church bathroom of all places!) and asked for forgiveness from God and from one another for past offenses. God was moving, and we had revival among the youth!

AUNT CATHERINE, GENEALOGY, AND JESUS

A friend of mine loved to research genealogy at the Marion Library. She wanted to research to see if any of my mother Violet's siblings were still living. She did some digging and found my Aunt Catherine was living in San Diego, California. I called my Aunt Catherine and told her who I was. I told her our son David was living in Los Angeles and we would love to see her while we were out visiting him. At first, she was a bit apprehensive, but I told her more details about myself. She agreed to a visit, and I was very happy to fly to meet my Aunt Catherine for the first time. We had such a lovely time. She commented at one point that she could see herself in me. That just thrilled my heart.

When I flew back to Indiana, Aunt Catherine and I became best friends on the telephone. We had so much in common, and she helped to fill in many of the gaps about our family tree for me. I loved her so much and continued to share the love of Christ with her. We were praying nightly as a family for her salvation. When the time seemed right, I shared the gospel with her and begged her to visit during our next revival meeting. Catherine said she'd come. She flew into Indianapolis and we picked her up for a visit in Marion.

All our children, now adults, visited with her at our home that week. Aunt Catherine attended the revival meetings and trusted in Christ for her salvation. She was in her 90s, but left Marion a gloriously changed woman for Jesus Christ.

We chatted every Saturday by phone. Sometime during our weekly conversation, I'd ask her, "Aunt Catherine, how is it with your soul?" Aunt Catherine assured me she was so glad she had met the true and living Lord and was bound for heaven. Although she had attended church in the past, she had never heard the gospel message. Aunt Catherine enjoyed her new-found relationship with Jesus that included daily Bible reading and prayer that ushered her all the way to Glory.

MARION MOSAICS

In addition to the older adult Sunday school, I also helped teach the college Sunday school class. In reality, I think those students taught me. Several of them were true Bible scholars.

Dwight enjoyed pastoring alongside Dave at Lakeview. After he was the youth pastor, Dwight served as the college pastor. He ministered to students from both Taylor University and Marion College. They loved him.

Some have said that the will of God is like looking at the back side of an ornate rug. Often, we can't make sense of the design, texture, or mosaic from the bottom side of it. We see only the rough threads and occasional outlines.

From heaven's perspective, however, a beautiful and intricate rug is clearly evident once we see it from the other side.

Looking back over our years in ministry, we often saw only threads and outlines of what God was weaving and designing in our lives and in the lives of others. As the years have progressed, I have been given glimpses of the wonderful design of the mosaic God has crafted in and through our lives. I am overwhelmed how Jesus has woven it together into a seamless work of art.

Yes, God's plans weren't always evident. They weren't always what we might have chosen or desired. But God always knew best. Heaven will echo for eternity the testimony of those who trusted Him, as they proclaim, "God does all things well!"

12

WASHINGTON, MICHIGAN

A CALL TO COMMUNITY WESLEYAN

Lakeview Church was growing and thriving with many new people visiting and joining. As much as we loved the people, the ministry, and the neighborhood we settled into, God was asking us to move once again.

Several said to us in the process, "Why would you leave? The church is doing so well." We didn't understand what God was doing, but as we learned to do long before then, we obeyed. God had always been trustworthy in such things, so we told Lakeview Church we were leaving.

We got a call from Community Wesleyan Church just outside of Detroit, Michigan. It was a county church on 26th Road that needed some healing. Believing God wanted us to be a part of that process, we accepted the call and moved once again into a church parsonage.

It was 1989, and just Dave and I for a time. I felt a bit lost without our family around and no kids. Marcia and Garry were in Plymouth, Indiana. Three years earlier, Dwight had married Dawn (Cheesman), and they were now living in Marion. David was singing with the music group, The Imperials, and touring all over the United States and even to some other countries.

Community Wesleyan Church (Now called Stoney Creek Community Church) was a lovely group of believers. I met some great people there, and they remain dear friends today.

In addition to church ministry, Dave and I did a lot of new things as "empty nesters." The church had a group who enjoyed bowling and playing golf. So, Dave and I learned to do both! Bowling and golf served as great ministry opportunities at the church, and also great outlets for us as we got closer to retiring from church ministry. Those sports continued to bring us great joy and helped keep our bodies moving well for years to come.

DENISE AND THE POWER OF PRAYER

I remember one Sunday morning when a young woman was kneeling at the altar of our church. She was obviously in great distress. I might have even heard her crying softly. Her name was Denise. I'll let her tell the story of what happened in her own words:

> One Sunday morning, I was praying and crying at the altar with my friend Diane. I was pregnant for the fourth time and experiencing distressing symptoms just as I had when I miscarried three previous times.
>
> My doctor had no solutions. He could offer no reasons as to why I couldn't carry a baby to full-term. He suggested genetic testing in the event I lost this fourth baby. I was discouraged to the point of believing I could never have a baby. My husband and I began initial inquiries into adoption.
>
> This time, only our parents and two friends, Diane and her husband, knew I was pregnant. It was just too painful to announce a pregnancy to other family and friends, only to later have to tell them we lost our baby.
>
> As Diane and I prayed that morning, our pastor's wife,

Miss Agnes, was praying at the altar further down from us. She had no idea what we were praying about. But suddenly she looked over at us. She got up and walked in our direction. She came over and laid her hand on my shoulder. She leaned over and whispered to me, `It has been placed on my heart to tell you that you will receive a miracle.'

With that she went back and sat down. I was shocked. I could not even think of anything to say in reply to Miss Agnes' statement! After a few days, my symptoms disappeared and seven months later, I gave birth to a beautiful, healthy baby girl.

We had received our miracle, just as Miss Agnes had said! In fact, we called our daughter our 'miracle baby.' And two years later, my husband and I were blessed with the birth of our son. I never had any problems with a full-term pregnancy again following that Sunday morning prayer!

Decades later, Denise once again recalled the impact that Sunday morning had on her life:

Each time I read this story it hits me even harder. I can testify to the fact God answers prayer and miracles do happen. I have the living proof in my beautiful 29-year old daughter. I still get goose bumps when I think back on Miss Agnes' words to me that beautiful Sunday morning. I know God is good... all the time.

RUBY, RUBBLE, AND A QUICK CUP OF COFFEE

I had been asked to speak to a group located much farther north than where we lived in Michigan. Because the area was close to where I lived as a child, I was determined to try and find my long-lost sister. Some years earlier, I was told my last name had been Bashaw. I discovered a

Ruby Bashaw in the phone book and learned she worked at a small factory. I drove to the factory and enter the office area. I explained to the receptionist that I was Ruby's sister and asked if I could see her.

A manager dispatched Ruby and told her I was there. Because I was on my way to a speaking engagement, I was all dressed up. Ruby, because she was hard at work at the factory, emerged wearing worn-out, dirty work clothes. It seemed our clothing became a metaphor of how differently our lives had gone and who we had become. The factory management kindly gave us two hours to leave and have coffee together.

Our time together was awkward and sad. Ruby was not a happy person. She seem to carry a sense of shame over the way her life had turned out. Ruby may have had a good heart, but her attitude, demeanor, and behavior was mean-spirited. I knew I didn't want that kind of life.

Let me explain. When I was taken from the orphanage, the people who took me out told me I had a sister. That was news to me. As I wrote earlier, I had no understanding what it meant to have a blood-relative like a brother or sister and was unaware that my actual brothers and sister were living with me at the orphanage.

When my aunt and uncle rescued me from the orphanage, they also wanted to find and rescue Ruby if possible. They eventually found her and discovered she was working as a nanny for some well-to-do people. The people owned cabins in the area as well as a grocery store. Ruby had been hired to watch their children (she was about 10 years older than me). When my aunt and uncle located Ruby, they asked her if she wanted to go home with them. However, seeing the person she had become, they didn't feel it was the best and healthiest idea for Ruby to live at their home. Instead, they found another place for her.

Unfortunately, there was a man living in that home at the time who was not a good person. Sadly, and before anyone knew it, she married him. It turned out to be a disastrous choice for Ruby. He treated her terribly and eventually they divorced. It was the beginning of a long and tragic downhill slide for my sister.

Back to our coffee visit …

Ruby lowered her coffee cup to the table and lifted her eyes to mine. "Agnes," she said, "I don't live like you do. The man I'm living with right now is not my husband. The truth is, I have five children from five different men."

Ruby reminded me of the woman at the well in John's Gospel. She too had been married five times and the man she was currently living with wasn't her husband either. And like the Samaritan woman Jesus met that day, my sister had been trying to quench the thirsting of her soul with the affection of men instead of the love of God. It was a path that left Ruby tired, discouraged, empty, and alone.

To my regret, that would be the last time I would see Ruby. I tried to share with her the love of Christ. I knew if she would only have ears to hear, it would wholeheartedly change her life. Looking back, I reflected many times on the fact that, outside of God's amazing grace, I too may have taken many of the rut-filled and ruinous roads my sister Ruby traveled.

A TERRIBLE FALL, A GRACIOUS AND HEALING GOD

When we moved from Indiana, I transferred my realtor's license in order to sell homes in Michigan. One Sunday, I got a call to show a house. Actually, it was a mansion. I had made a promise to the Lord long ago that I would not sell and show real estate on Sunday. But, in a weaker moment, my eyes saw the money I would make on that sale, and I broke my promise (I later confessed it all to the Lord!).

I went to the house showing and took a young lady who worked for a doctor friend of mine with me. I always wore high heels as a part of my professional attire. As we started down the stairs from the second floor of this sizable estate, my heel caught the carpet and down I went… about 33 steps worth of down… right to the front door. The young lady who was with me told me to take off my coat.

"Why?" I asked.

"Because I think you broke your arm!" she replied.

We got the coat off, and my arm was not okay! My young friend wanted to call the ambulance. I said she could drive my car and get me to the hospital in Rochester (Michigan) just as fast. "Call my husband and let him know what happened," I told her. "Then, let's go!"

We got to the hospital ahead of Dave. When he arrived, the staff questioned him about what had happened. Because women sometimes come to the emergency room as victims of domestic abuse, they wanted to check out my story. I guess I looked like I had been beaten up!

The doctors took a lot of x-rays. I found out my elbow was sticking out, and it was broken badly. They told us I needed to have surgery to repair my arm. During surgery, the doctor told me I would keep my arm but I would never be able to use it. I let him know we served a great God and that He was a God who could do miracles!

After a few days in the hospital, they let me come home. Marcia had driven up from Indiana and was there to help me as I recovered. I couldn't take the medicine they gave me; it was too strong. I remember staring out the kitchen window one morning and crying out—the pain was excruciating. I looked out and saw two robins walking on the sidewalk near our back door. I knew God was aware of my love for robins. My mind recalled God's promise in the Bible to care for the lilies and birds, and I sensed Him saying, "I got you, Agnes. I will get us through this!"

I began to slowly heal. Pain was constantly an issue because my body has never been able to tolerate strong medicine. The chiropractor I saw was quite helpful in the healing process.

A lot of peaks and valleys of recovery followed. In all, I had to endure nine subsequent surgeries. They were painful. Greater still was the pain of knowing I could no longer play the piano as I once had. Times of personal enjoyment, accompanying others, and playing in worship services seemed to be gone forever.

Grief over not playing could have sunk me low. I remembered and affirmed, however, what God had done many times over in my life and in the lives of others: God answers prayer! Many family members and church friends began praying earnestly for God to heal my arm.

Then, during a worship service one Sunday morning, I felt led to go forward and play the piano. I wrestled with God and that thought for just a moment. I knew my movement and dexterity was severely limited. I didn't want to embarrass God or myself.

But I had heard God's speaking. I had walked and talked with God too long to know that what was being directed was from Him. So, I went forward, sat down at the piano, and began to play.

As if my arm had never been broken, my hands moved effortlessly up and down the keyboard. The music rang out, with what sounded to me, like the melody of angels. I could play again! The Lord had restored my arm and hand.

Several people remarked that I was now playing better than I ever had. I could only laugh in joy and delight at how good the Lord had been to me!

SURPRISED BY LOVE

All of the churches we served blessed us in so many ways, Community Wesleyan among them. One time, in a message I gave at the church, I shared the details of getting married to Dave in my parents' living room and how our honeymoon was less than ideal. Lovingly, the church surprised us with a big wedding and reception. It was beyond imagination and more than we could have ever afforded as newlyweds. The church even flew our kids in for the celebration. What a great surprise! What a wonderful blessing!

BASKING IN GOD'S PRESENCE

One Sunday morning, I was sitting in the choir loft with the rest of the choir. After singing the anthem for the day, the rest of the choir made their way down to sit with their family and friends. But I remained. God was speaking to me, and I wanted to listen and take it all in. I was looking up to heaven, enjoying the presence of the Lord, and longing to hear more from Jesus. Dave continued the service while I stood and basked in God's presence.

Friends later told me I stood there for over 15 minutes as the service continued. Then, I heard the Lord say, "Agnes, you belong to Me. You are My own!" Hearing all I needed to hear God say that morning, I opened my eyes, and gently walked to my seat on the front pew.

* * *

TEN-FINGER PRAYERS PAUSE:
WORSHIP PRAYERS

My need of God has been great throughout my life. And, I've never hesitated to ask God for things only He can do and provide. As a loving Father, God wants and invites us to come to Him in our time of need.

God is good and kind to provide for, care for, heal, protect, and guide us... and, God is so much more than someone who meets *our* needs. The King of kings and Lord of lords—the One who hung the stars, makes the sun to shine, the oceans to rise, formed you and me out of clay and put air in our lungs—is worthy of our highest worship and awe. After all, we are servants in God's Kingdom; God is not a servant or subject in ours.

So, we worship God. Not because we *have to*, but because we *get to!* We were actually made for this. And while we are commanded to "worship God and Him only" (Luke 4:8 and Deuteronomy 6:13), why wouldn't we want to worship and adore the God who dotes over us, calls us His very own children, and sees us as the apple of His eye?!

So, worship God and make prayer a part of your worship. You may not get "lost in wonder, love, and praise" in the same manner I did on that one Sunday morning in the choir loft. You don't have to. You were made to uniquely worship God in ways that look and feel just like you.

Here's what I know, if you put your whole heart and self into genuinely loving and worshipping God—making *God* the focus of your worship and prayer—God will be so pleased with your offering!

Just let your heart, mind, body, and soul express in some way what those around God's throne in the Book of Revelation keep saying, singing, and believing. Why not try it on for size right now...

Let your heart go, your prayers ascend, your love express...

> *"Holy, holy, holy*
> *is the Lord God Almighty,*
> *who was, and is, and is to come."*
>
> — REVELATION 4:8

Fall down before him who sits on the throne and worship him who lives for ever and ever. Lay *your* crown before the throne and say:

> *"You are worthy, our Lord and God,*
> *to receive glory and honor and power,*
> *for you created all things,*
> *and by your will they were created*
> *and have their being."*
>
> — REVELATION 4:10-11

* * *

DENVER

GOD MOVES MOUNTAINS AND BOXES

When I put the Christmas decorations away after the new year, my custom for many years was to pray and ask the Lord if I needed to pack the decorations in their boxes "secure for moving" or "lightly packed" and ready for the next Christmas celebration at our present location. Praying such things isn't unusual for pastoral families. Talks and plans by churches and pastors often begin the first part of the year.

God's message was clear to me one post-Christmas decoration packing day. God relayed, "Pack them for a move." I told Dave we would be moving, and he said, "I don't think so. At least not yet, because we still have another year left."

Soon after, Dave had a church board meeting. During the meeting, the Lord spoke to Dave. God let Dave know his present assignment was over and that we would be moving. Dave came home and said, "We're moving!" (I wasn't surprised!)

The year was 1994. Our son, Dwight, and his lovely wife, Dawn, invited us to move to Denver, Colorado to minister alongside them at Kingdom Building Ministries,* a ministry God led Dwight to begin in 1986.

The call and ministry need was to serve as "Pastors to the Staff," which we accepted.

> *While Kingdom Building Ministry changed their name to Forge (ForgeForward.org) in 2014, the mission has remained the same from the beginning: "to multiply a movement of more Kingdom laborers who live with hearts on fire for Jesus and lives on purpose by advancing God's Kingdom in every facet and sphere of society worldwide through Itinerant Preaching, Practical Equipping, and Kingdom Resources."*

KINGDOM CALL CONDO

When we moved to Denver, we found a condominium for sale and thought it was the one God had for us. We went to the sales office, and while we were writing our offer, I felt like God said to offer higher than the listed price. We did, and when the realtor came back into the room, she said there was two other offers, but we had gone higher. They accepted our offer.

I was sure God was leading us, and we have lived in this condo God provided the whole time we have lived in Denver. We have a great patio view of a long, beautiful, golf green that overlooks the the snow-capped Rocky Mountains in the distance. The view of the mountains and snow that remains year-round is majestic and reminds us daily how big God is, how beautiful He's made us, and who's really in charge.

PERRY AND BUTLER REAL ESTATE

I obtained my Colorado real estate license and began working for Century 21, but the office was several miles away. A lady I knew worked for a real estate company called *Perry & Butler* that was close to my home, so I talked to the manager, and they wanted me to start as soon as I could. I really enjoyed my time there. What I liked about real estate was that I could set my own hours and take days off when I wanted to go someplace. Dwight and Dawn lived close to us, and we would often babysit for Dara and Dreyson (their children, our grandchildren) while

Dwight and Dawn were away on preaching assignments and ministry trips. I rarely said no to caring for the kids—one, because I know they felt safe with me; and two, well, they're our grandkids!

On one grandkid-watching occasion, Dara set the burglar alarm without knowing it. During the night, I got up to go downstairs. The motion detector tripped and the alarm blared. It scared me so bad! The police were there in minutes, and I told them what had happened. *At least we know it works!* I remember joking to myself.

When I sat with Dwight and Dawn's kids, I daily experienced new things and looked at every challenge with awe and imagination. As an older person, I would wish I still had that quality. I realize that life is so fleeting that you don't want to waste a single moment of your life. Every season has a time and purpose.

Memories with Dara and Dreyson growing up were precious! I taught Dara how to knit—something she still does today. Dreyson and his buddy would police the neighborhood in the evening and kindly check to see if anyone needed help. It served as good training. Now, he's grown up and is in the Marines. He still patrols places to keep our country safe and continues to do whatever is necessary to help people with whatever they need.

When Dreyson was in high school, he played basketball. Dave and I would go to his games and cheer him on.

At Christmas time, Dawn would bake cookies and treats to give out. We'd go home to home in the neighborhood, sing carols, and hand out our baked treats. The neighbors loved it. And we love doing it.

ORPHANAGE BOARD

I served many years on the board of Abenezer Children's Home, an orphanage in Ethiopia that ministered to over 60 kids. We kept records of the children's ever-changing clothes sizes and were able to keep them well-clothed throughout the year through generous donations. One year, Costco donated jackets for all the kids.

The orphans suffered some pretty harsh realities and shared many heartbreaking stories. They were so appreciative we took them in. We were thrilled we could help. It did my heart good to know I could minister to kids in ways I never experienced growing up in an orphanage. God never wastes our time—regardless of our tragedies and tough spots.

LOVE CAME DOWN AT CHRISTMAS

At Christmas time, Forge would have a night of fun, food, and gifts for the staff. Forge leadership appreciated the staff's year-round work for the Kingdom and wanted to celebrate and appreciate them.

Several years at our Christmas gathering, staff families would gather their children and ask me to tell them "the orange story" from my childhood. I'd share the story about how a Christmas orange became my toy and make-believe friend. Other times, I'd share the story about how I made a toy out of an old rag or handkerchief and how I made it come to life like a puppet. Those nights were special, and we had such a great time of fellowship.

Several Saturdays before Christmas we had a day where we'd watch all the staff family's kids so the parents could have a day to Christmas shop all by themselves. I would ask the older girls to help babysit the younger ones. We didn't charge the families anything—it was our Christmas gift to them! I always had two or three dollars to share with the girls that helped. The kids look forward to those special Saturdays.

THE POWER OF LITTLE THINGS

Our pastor in Denver preached one time on "The Power of Little Things." He said little things can become big things and we should never underestimate them. That's wonderful news when we're talking about mustard seeds and a little faith to move mountains. But when the pastor began talking about the power of "little" sins, the Holy Spirit really began to convict me.

My mind immediately raced back to the time I stole a lollipop at the orphanage. I never told anyone, and it had been plaguing me for years. I thought to myself, *I can't go and make restitution; the orphanage no longer exists!* So, I asked the Lord what to do. He gave me the answer: "Put a dollar in the offering plate every Sunday until I tell you to stop." And that's what I did. Sunday after Sunday I obediently and joyfully did what God asked of me.

Finally, after putting yet another dollar bill in the offering one Sunday morning, I clearly hear the Lord say, "Okay, Agnes, you can stop now."

So that's what I did. I felt free from it all. Satan was no longer using a stolen lollipop to make a sucker out of me!

I took a minute to add up how costly sin can be as I counted the number of weeks I put dollar bills in the offering plate. In addition to years of guilt I suffered over my transgression, I figured the sin of my lollipop thievery cost me $42!

THE APPLE OF GOD'S EYE

On another occasion, a preacher was sharing about what it means to be "the apple of God's eye." As a practical way of applying this truth, the preacher sent an apple home with everyone listening and gave this instruction: "Don't eat the apple until you really know and believe that you are the apple of God's eye!"

I took the assignment seriously. I put the apple in my refrigerator to keep. Several times over the next week I looked at the apple, but I couldn't say the words. I knew they were true. In fact, I especially knew they were true for other people (and given the occasion, I'd let them know in an instant). But years of feeling unwanted and unloved, though decades ago, made it difficult to believe how much God loved, doted over, and wanted *me*.

Later in the week, I was sitting on a bench outside the hospital. Dave was going through some pretty rough cancer issues at the time. I remember praying for Dave and sensing God so near. God's love overwhelmed me.

Without thought, I opened my purse. There was the apple I had gotten from the refrigerator! My encounter with God let me know in my heart what I knew to be true in my understanding. "Jesus, I believe I am the apple of your eye. Thank you! Thank you! Thank you for loving me so much and so well!" And with that, I took my first bite.

* * *

TEN-FINGER PRAYER PAUSE:
EVERYDAY PRAYERS

An apple, a refrigerator, a purse, a park bench. These were the everyday objects surrounding my profound encounter with God as He reminded me, "Agnes, you're the apple of My eye!" It's not that the pastor, our church, or Sunday morning worship didn't matter. They do. Immensely! It's just I'm amazed at how often profound prayer moments in my life have come in the everyday pitter-patter of life. Prayer as I changed diapers. Prayer as I drove to work. Prayer as I walked the neighborhood or bent to retrieve my golf ball after sinking a putt. I've learned that the best place to pray is wherever I am. Why? Because that's where God is!

It took me a large part of my life to shake the religious notion that prayer was reserved for special times and special places. Churches, worship services, revivals, and retreats—those all seemed like the appropriate venues for prayer. When someone was in trouble, a meal was to be eaten, a loved one died, a friend needed healing, or a sin required confessing—those seemed like the times to pray.

Can I let you in on a secret? I've discovered the more time I spent with God in prayer, the more I realize He cares about every aspect and detail of my life. What's more, God wants me to know more and more the details of *His* life and what He is up to in His Kingdom and what's going on all around me. God wants me to enjoy the ice cream I'm licking and talk to Him about it—because God loves good things and wants me to love them too. God wants me to be aware of the person near me who was hurting—because when they hurt, God hurts too and maybe He wants me to whisper a word of encouragement to them on His behalf.

Everyday moments, every day, wherever we find ourself—those are the times and places God wants us to have conversation with Him. Those are the moments God wants to talk, listen, and share with us. Those are the times He often instructs, delights, motivates, guides, and moves us into action.

I hope you'll practice prayer in your everyday moments. Enoch, who daily walked and talked with God, seemed to be pretty good at it (Genesis 5:24). So was Brother Lawrence, a man who talked often with God while washing dishes and repairing shoes.* I'm pretty sure as you practice God's presence through prayer in your everyday places, you will have a lifetime of God-moments to share.

> * A great book on Brother Lawrence and his life of prayer is
> *Practicing God's Presence: Brother Lawrence for Today's Reader*
> by Robert Elmer. I highly recommend it!

* * *

WHAT THE SURGEON SAID, WHAT GOD DID

When we moved to Denver, I still needed several more surgeries on my arm. They were performed at the Seventh-Day Adventist Hospital about 7 miles from our home. One particular surgery, they said I would have to stay in the hospital. I said I couldn't. They said I could take the machine for my arm home, but I would have to stay on the machine at least eight hours a day and only get off to go to the bathroom. Dave would have to fix some of the meals. That machine was my life for days! I would go back to the hospital for another surgery and come home hurting and crying and get back on the machine. After I was done with the machine, they came and got it. I was so glad it was gone!

For the next part of my recovery, I went to the indoor pool. It was less than a mile away and I'd be there first thing at 7 a.m. when it opened. I'd get in the small pool and put my arm in and try to move it around. It hurt, but I knew I needed to move it. I would go every morning and try to raise my hand out of the water.

It took a good three years to get my arm and hand moving right. The

surgeon had said I would never be able to use it, but God said I would…
if I continue to exercise it. So, I did!

After a lot of prayer, hard work, and exercise, my arm and hand was
fully functional. I was so excited and grateful to God! The doctor's
nurse called me one day and asked for a picture of me using my arm
because they couldn't believe I could use it. I was happy to take that
picture and show them what God had done!

A FOURSOME AND FAMILY DISCOVERY

The doctor thought Dave's and my love for golf was a good way to keep
my arms strong. It was fun to be in the great outdoors on beautiful golf
courses, and especially so in Colorado. One day, we didn't have a
foursome with us and the course was overcrowded. So, they asked if we
would allow a couple to play with us. We said that would be fine. The
other two of our newly formed foursome was a mother and daughter.
The course being crowded meant times of waiting at just about every
hole. So, as golfers are prone to do, we talked with our new friends as
we waited for our turn on the tee.

We discovered in our conversation that they were from Munsing,
Michigan.

"I am sure you don't know him," I said, "but I have a brother in
Munsing who I've been wanting to meet up with."

"What's his name?" she asked.

"Edward Bashaw," I replied.

Her mouth dropped wide open. "Edward Bashaw!" she said. "He's
our next-door neighbor!"

We couldn't believe it! Isn't that just like God to send folks all the
way from Michigan to Denver to deliver an answer of prayer for me?!
And God used a crowded golf course and mixed up foursome to do it!

I told my new friend that I had several brothers but didn't know
where they were. I explained to her I was "the black sheep of the family"
and asked her if, when she went home, she would please tell Ed that she
had met me.

With this newly opened door, I was determined as ever to go to the

Upper Peninsula of Michigan to find the orphanage, the court house that held my birth certificate I had never seen, and my long-lost brother, Edward.

DAVE WENT WEST, I WENT INVESTIGATING

A year later, I sent Dave on a fun father-son trip to visit David in California. Marcia and I decided we wanted just the two of us to take a trip to upper Michigan to dig around and discover some things about my past.

Our starting point was Marcia's house in Plymouth. The morning we were to leave, it was raining. Garry, my son-in-law, felt uneasy about that. He called from his office and said he was going too. At first, I was disappointed that it wasn't just Marcia and me. It was a real blessing, however, that Garry came. He was such a blessing as our driver.

Garry navigated us to the orphanage where I spent a number of my childhood years. When we arrived, we found the orphanage as expected —boarded up and abandoned. Garry searched around and found a way for us to enter.

There I stood in the six-story building of my past. Memory after memory flooded my mind. It was austere. It was haunting. I saw the stairs leading to the basement, but I couldn't bring myself to take them. A nauseous feeling flooded my gut. My body became suddenly aware of an event so egregious that my mind thought it best to forget.

Marcia had done a lot of checking about the orphanage and located the building where all the records were kept: The Marquette County Museum. We visited the building, and on the second floor, a lady found files about the orphanage that we could read while we were there, but making copies was absolutely forbidden (there were definitely events and stories they never wanted to get out). The record keeper started talking to us and let us know that her husband was in that orphanage too. She also said he never wanted to talk about it.

We read for a while, and the lady came back and handed us some papers. She whispered while nodding toward the papers, "You can make copies of these. Exit this outside door and go down the stairs. There'll be a copier there. Please be careful—if you get caught, I will get fired." We thanked her greatly!

We continued our quest by searching for my birth certificate in several county court houses in the area. Our sleuthing led us to the Crystal Falls Court house. After a lot of digging, they found my dust-covered birth record in the attic. They gave us a copy. To my astonishment, I discovered I was actually two years older than I thought I was for all these years.

The "aha" and "can you believe that" moments of the day continued when I looked across the hall from the records department and realized I was looking into the court room where the judge released me once and for all from having to go back to the orphanage. I gave thanks to God and for Uncle Ernest who came to fight for my freedom.

We made our final stop at the Catholic adoption agency to inquire if they had any information on my childhood. They informed us they really weren't in a position to help. In my heart, I knew there were, so I said, "We can't leave until you give us some help." After a few calls and side conversations, they told us that if we would give them our contact information, they would call us later and mail some stuff.

Feeling that was the best we could do, we took their offer. Two weeks later, we got a call to tell us they would be sending things. Then they added, "... but you will need to see a counselor after you read them." They were serious, but it made me laugh—because in my family, we have three counselors!

Well, the package came. I called Dave to come home from the office, and we opened it together. It was some sad stuff, but we were ready for it and learned a lot about my family.

I also found out information about me are on a disk filed at Notre Dame. Those things have yet to be opened or discovered. With the orphanage now closed, I could only wonder about the stories and discoveries left untold of the 200 boys and girls I journeyed with at the orphanage.

FACING THE PAST, GOD MAKES ALL THINGS NEW

Our hopes in "going back" were to discover some places of healing, locate my birth certificate, and reunite with my brother Edward. We had done the first two, now it was on to see my brother.

I called Edward at his home in Munsing, and asked if I could speak with him. His voice was gentle and our conversation was kind. He invited us to come over for coffee.

We arrived at Edward's house and our time was there was precious. So many things to catch up on and questions to ask. We knew it could never be done over one evening of coffee.

Still, we did our best to hear about each other's families and where life had taken us all these years apart. Among many other things, I told him about Dwight and David singing on the "Day of Discovery" television program, which I thought he might be interested in watching. I found out later that he did watch it—a lot!—and was excited to tell others about his nephews on TV. He never missed a show.

Edward and I exchanged a lot of phone calls and letters after our meeting. It's hard to explain the joy of having connection with my blood brother. Without a lot of words, I'll just say it was special and deeply meaningful.

Some time later, I felt led to write him a letter about his relationship with God. I wrote to him about how I was glad we reconnected and how I had found joy in my life. I shared the gospel message and explained how he too could be a Christian. I also sent him a gospel tract with a prayer of commitment in it. I pray he read the letter and trusted Jesus. I never got a response—he passed away two weeks later.

FORGING FORWARD!

Dave and I moved to minister with Forge's staff nearly three decades ago. We loved on them, carried their burdens in prayer, and were available to counsel with them as needed. It was a ministry God called us to and we have loved ever since!

I hope you'll get on Forge's website (ForgeForward.org) and learn about all about the ways God has impacted lives since 1986. At the time of this writing, over one million people have heard the life-changing gospel all around the world through Forge itinerate speakers. Of those, over 350,000 said "yes" to making Jesus Christ the Lord and Savior of their life! Thousands more have been equipped to multiply Kingdom laborers in over 100 different countries. All this, and so much more! Maybe you're one who has been impacted by God through Forge. I certainly hope so.

It's hard to believe that an orphan from upper Michigan could be used by God in such great Kingdom work, but it's true. I have been. God has used me and Dave in unimaginable ways for His Kingdom sake at Forge. Not because we're great, but because God is!

And God will use you too for His Kingdom right where you live. Just pray to the Lord and say something like, "Lord, here I am. I'm available. What would You like me to do?"

Great things God has done! Great things He is doing! And we give Him all the praise!

TEN-FINGER PRAYER PAUSE:
INTERCESSORY PRAYERS

As I look back over the expanse of my life, I am overwhelmed at God's goodness. God rescued me as an orphan and blessed me with a loving family. He healed my body and mended the deepest wounds of my heart. He turned my sorrows to laughter and many griefs to joy. He called me worthy and provided all I needed to serve His Kingdom.

Included in God's blessings for me were the number of people who diligently prayed me for along the way. People I knew—like my My Aunt Carrie, Ortha and Earnest, my Mom and Dad, and a number of spiritual brothers and sisters from many churches, places, and spaces. And then, there were a host of people I never knew who prayed for me. They lifted me by name before the Father out of their love for Him...

and their love for me. They counted it a joy to lift my needs, concerns, decisions, and dreams before the Lord. They took seriously I Timothy 2:1-4:

> I urge, then, first of all, that petitions, prayers, intercession and thanksgiving be made for all people—for kings and all those in authority, that we may live peaceful and quiet lives in all godliness and holiness.

They knew that "all people" meant *all* people. So, they prayed for those they knew and those they didn't, those who were lovable and those who were trouble. They prayed for friends and enemies, for church members and gang members, preachers and politicians, princesses and paupers... and they prayed for orphans just like me.

No wonder my life calling was a call to pray. How could I not pray for others—those I know and those I don't—when so many have prayed for me? I couldn't think of a better way to say "thank you" to God for all He's done in my life than to pray for others who need the presence and power of our gracious God.

You might not have a lifelong calling to prayer in the same manner as God has given me (and then again, you might!). But you have been called to pray for others—to intercede on their behalf. To ask the Father to do in them, for them, and on behalf of them what they cannot do for themselves.

Have you considered lately who you might intercede for in prayer? If you aren't sure, just ask God to show you. He will. You need not open your eyes and look around long before you see someone who needs a touch from the Lord. The needs are many—those willing to pray are few. Why not get started on being a part of someone's answered prayer and blessing by praying for them today!

* * *

PEARLS GAINED

God has been so gracious to meet me at every twist and turn of life. And there have been many. Here are just a few of the many "pearls" I've gained along the way as I've leaned into the Him who "changest not," and whose "compassions fail not." God's faithfulness has been, and continues to be, "great unto me."

ENCOURAGEMENT BLOWS WIND INTO FLAT SAILS

Every place we lived, we found people who were lonely and need of encouragement and love. I realized that maybe I could be that for them. I remember a Bessie Hicks, who was pretty much deaf, and she would come to my house and just wanted to talk. She was not a Christian, but she started coming to church. Could I be her friend just living out what God has done for me? Could I "brighten her corner?"

I remember Millie, the restaurant owner, who once told me she "hated the woman at church who always had a smile." I said, "Millie, I'm coming up to your restaurant. Get the coffee on because I have a great story to tell you!" I told her more about the woman who always had a smile—how her husband would beat her and lock her out of her house, and how she would go to the back of the church and sleep. How could I encourage that woman and Millie, who didn't take the time to get to know her?

Could I be a mother figure to a young mother of two, who had no mother herself? Could I be the one a wife could call when her husband had a bad accident?

Could I be the encourager to a couple of young boys who wanted me to get in a boat and go whitewater rafting? Boys who are now college graduates and great Christians who never forgot my time with them?

Every move of God needs an encourager. Constantly ask, "Who needs an encouraging word from God (and me) today?"

JOY IS CONTAGIOUS

I remember meeting a lonely, adolescent girl, whose dad was an alcoholic, just like mine had been. I did whatever I could to convey to her she had value in God's eyes. Our friendship has continued through the decades.

Just recently, she wrote something beautiful on her Facebook page. She shared how God had helped her to attain so many things she thought she could never accomplish in life. Through our friendship, she met the Lord Jesus and grew up to be a really wonderful person.

Never underestimate how God can bring, grow, and sustain joy in others through our love, presence, and encouragement.

FORGIVENESS BRINGS FREEDOM

I will be honest and admit that it took a long time for me to forgive my birth father. Even now, there are times I'm tempted to be bitter in my heart toward him. I never knew anything but his cruelty, ferocious temper, and violence when he was drunk.

But how can I not forgive my birth father when God has so graciously and generously forgiven me? Forgiveness is not always easy, but as we're able to humbly, honestly, and sincerely say to someone, "I forgive you," it does provide a lot of peace and freedom.

NOTHING IS WASTED, NOT EVEN IN ORPHANAGES

All these years later, I harbor no bitterness regarding the orphanage. Clearly, it wasn't a good place. That said, it did teach me certain useful disciplines—like getting up early, brushing my teeth, and creating routines and rhythms.

The disciplines of the orphanage eventually helped me in my spiritual life as well. For instance, the rhythms of daily mass and prayer times, though religiously skewed, helped me establish good devotional practices later in life. Now, I have rhythms of *wanting* to be with God, not *having* to. I wake up in the morning and my first thought is, "It's time to be with Jesus and in God's Word!"

Then there was the practice of being obedient. If I was given an assignment by one of the nuns, I didn't say, "Oh wait, Sister, I'll get to in a bit." Not a chance! I had to do what they told me, when they told me. That helped me later in life to do what God was asking with quicker response.

Don't ever think God is wasting your time. He isn't. God is always at work—making things whole, bringing things to life—even in life's most awkward, unlikely, and sometimes unlovely places and events.

GOD RESTORES THE BROKENHEARTED

The Psalmist was no stranger to a broken heart. He wrote,

> "Though You have made me see troubles, many and bitter, you will restore my life again; from the depths of the earth, you will again bring me up. You will increase my honor and comfort me once more." —Psalm 71: 20-21

People sometimes ask me, "Agnes, with all the sorrows and tragedies of your early life, how is it you didn't become bitter and angry at God and others as an adult, as many others do?"

That's a good question. I know people who experienced so much sorrow and heartbreak in their lives as children that as adults they all but given up on God. Thankfully, by God's grace and mercy, that's not my story. Nor does it have to be yours—regardless of what you have been through as a child or as an adult.

The only way I can explain the amazing transformation in my life is that God gave me a sliver of hope while I was in the orphanage. And when He freed me from that place, it burst wide open. After I left the orphanage, I began to realize there was a different way, a higher way, a brighter way, a better way than what I had known before.

Sometimes the slightest ray of God's hope in one's heart is all that's needed to find the life and restoration God desires.

LAUGHTER IS A SECRET WEAPON

The orphanage taught me the secret weapon of laughter. When kids would laugh at me, I would laugh too. Laughing with them seem to disarm them and usually made them stop. On a few occasions, it actually turned them from being my enemy to being my friend.

I tell my grandchildren this advice even now. When you are teased, just laugh with those who are laughing at you. At the very least, it usually gets them to stop. At most, you might make a new friend.

I believe God gives us laughter. I think it reflects His loving, joy-filled heart. And I believe when we laugh, God joins us.

SORROW LASTS FOR A NIGHT, JOY FOREVER

I saw in my relatives who rescued me from the orphanage a joy I had never known before. The more I saw it in them, the more I wanted it for myself. My aunts and uncles seemed to have more joy in a single day than I experienced in an entire year.

Eventually, I learned that the joy they had wasn't something to earn or learn, it was something to receive and share. It was a joy that only God can provide; it fills our hearts and then overflows to others.

If joy is something attractive to you—something you want more of—I can tell you how to get it... get up-close to Jesus. The more you know Him, the more joy will flood your heart and life.

THE WAY OF LOVE MAKES HEARTS SHINE

I've made it a goal in life never to be mean to anyone. While I'm not afraid to stick up for myself or to tell people what I believe, I am also determined never to be ugly or mean. Meanness doesn't reflect God's heart; love does. A mean person is not an attractive person, and being mean is never an enticement for a non-believer to follow Christ. Anyone I know that really loves Jesus was attracted to love, not meanness.

I think it's important to put away anger and meanness and instead look for the good in others and love them the best we know how. Walt Whitman, the great American poet, once said, "Keep your face always toward the sunshine and shadows will fall behind you." More and more, I want to live the brighter way. I determined some time ago to keep my face toward toward Jesus. I believe if I do that, I can't help but treat others with love and kindness. Life's just too short to be mean.

PRAYER CHANGES EVERYTHING!

Prayer changes things. It changes you, me, others, the situation, attitudes, outcomes, expectations… it brings comfort, insight, strength, power, forgiveness, transformation, and life.

Prayer isn't accessible just to the popular, powerful, intelligent, skilled, wealthy, or super spiritual. Prayer belongs to anyone willing to talk to God.

Prayer is powerful because God is. It puts us where God is at work and connects us to all God's resources.

Most of all, prayer puts us in God's presence. And there is no better place to be. In God's presence, we know more of who we are, what we are about, where we belong, what we are to do, where we're going, and how much we are loved.

Like I said, prayer changes everything!

CLOSING THOUGHTS

I wrote this book for my children, grandchildren, and great grandchildren to let them know how much God loves them, that they're the apple of His eye, that they matter immensely to Him, and that when they pray—God hears and speaks and acts.

I wrote to let them (and you) know, that when you face hard decisions, learn to wait on God—don't try to take control and fight your own battles. God is the one who fights them for us... and He will!

I wrote to counsel them (and you) to be patient and trust God. He does for us what we can't do for ourselves, and He's always right on time.

I wrote to caution them (and you) that while we are free to choose, we are not free from the consequences of our choices.

I wrote to challenge them (and you) to live by God's commands, walk in His ways, be available for His use, and get active in His Kingdom work.

I wrote to urge them (and you) to pray and to keep praying!

As you do these things and stay close to the heart of God, know this:

> God will bless you,
> your family,
> and many others
> for many generations to come
> and well into eternity.

Finally, remember this and never forget …

> God loves you!
> He wants the best for you!
> Nothing is impossible with Him!
> Blessed is the one who trusts in the Lord!

> What a life!
> Amen, Amen, and Amen!

FINAL CHALLENGE

What impossible things might God want to do in and through you as you yield your life to Him and pray? What new things might God want to do in *others* as you lift them to Him in prayer? What adventures with God might you take? What praises will you sing? What miracles will you see? What joys will you experience? … as you pray!

You've read the book. You've heard my story. Let's review Philippians 4:13 and the Ten-Finger Prayer once again:

I can do some things. Nope, not it.
I can do most things. Again, falls short.
I can do everything except this one thing. You know that's not the whole of it.

Whatever you're facing…
Wherever you've been…
Whoever has hurt you…
However overwhelming and unsolvable the situation…

No matter the size of the mountain...
Despite those who say you can't...
Regardless of feeling that God may have mistakenly called the
wrong person to the task...

Say it with me,

"I can do all things through Christ who strengthens me!"

I
Can
Do
All
Things
Through
Christ
Who
Strengthens
Me

It's true. It's true. It's true.

There's nothing so impossible that God can't make it possible.

Nothing so damaged or broken that God can't and won't make it new.

God's life, your best life, is in front of you... as you bend your knees,
humble your heart, elevate your eyes, lift your hands... and pray!

PHOTO ALBUM
LIFE ALONG THE WAY

1. Agnes' mom, Voilet; Agnes' aunts,
   Catherine and Ortha, and uncle, Ed.
2 & 3. Agnes' family before they
   were separated.
4. Nichols family reunion where
   Agnes meets Archie & Erma.
5. Agnes' mom and dad, Violet &
   Herbert Bashaw.

1. Bashaw children's first day at Good Will Farm.
2. Good Will Faram visit, 2010.
3. Good Will Farm fire escape.
4. Agnes at Good Will Farm.
5. Agnes and brother, Ed.

1. Holy Family Orphanage.
2 & 3. Holy Family Orphanage visit, 2010.
4. Holy Family Orphanage chapel.
5. Agnes and mother, Violet Bashaw.

1. Agnes Bashaw Nichols.
2-5. Agnes Nichols.

1. Agnes and Ron Nichols.
2. Nichols family–Erma, Agnes, Ron, Archie.
3 & 4. First home--Vassar, Michigan.
5. Ortha Nichols.

1. Ortha and Ernest Nichols.
2. Ortha Nichols and brother, Edward.
3. Dave Robertson.
4 & 5. Dave and Agnes Robertson.

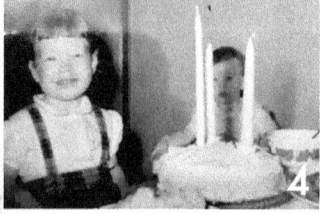

1 & 2, Dave, Agnes, and firstborn
   child, Marcia.
3 & 4. Dwight and Marcia.
5. Robertson vacation on Lake
   Maddock, Canada.

1-4. Agnes and Dave's children--Marcia, Dwight, David.
5. Robertson family.

1. Dave and Agnes.
2. Dave and Agnes' family: Garry & Marcia Lauber with their sons,
   Jeremiah & Landon; Dwight & Dawn Robertson; David Robertson.
3. Agnes with daughter, Marcia, and grandson, Jeremiah.
4. Agnes' brother, Ed Bashaw.
5. Agnes with daughter, Marcia, and Evelyn & Ed Bashaw.

1. Agnes and brother, Ed Bashaw.
2. Ed's four children: Kim, Kay, Tom, Karen.
3. Agnes and Dave.
4. Agnes four wheeling in her 70's.
5. Agnes' first grandchild, Jeremiah Lauber.

1. Agnes' family with grandchildren.
2. Dave & Agnes with sons, Dwight and David.
3. Robertson family.
4. Dave & Agnes; granddaughter, Dara, with her husband, Charlie Marquis.
5. Agnes' family.

1. Agnes' great granddaughters, Leighton and Selah Lauber.
2. Dwight Robertson with his grandson, Bowen.
3. Agnes' 90th birthday.
4. Dwight & Dawn Robertson with their son, Dreyson.
5. Dwight & Dawn with their children and spouses: Dreyson (son) & Shiloh and Dara (daughter) & Charlie Marquis.

1. Agnes and Dave dedicating their great grandson, Leighton Lauber.
2. Lisa Nichols, Ron Nichols, Theresa Nichols-Kessler, and Agnes at her
   brother Ed's funeral.
3. Agnes' first great grandchild, Leighton Lauber.
4. Agnes.
5. Garry and Marcia Lauber with their son, Landon, his wife, Samantha,
   and their children Ezekiel, Ezra, and Clementine.

1. Dave & Agnes with Dwight & Dawn and their children and spouses: Garry
   & Marcia Lauber, Dwight & Dawn Robertson, Dreyson & Shiloh Robertson.
2. Dave & Agnes.
3. Agnes.
4. Dave & Agnes.
5. Dave & Agnes' children: Marcia, Dwight, David.

1. Dave & Agnes.
2. Dave & Agnes' children: Dwight, David, Marcia.
3. Archie & Erma Nichols.
4. Agnes with her son, Dwight.
5. Dave & Agnes.

1. Dave & Agnes.
2. Agnes.
3. Dave & Agnes.
4. Dave & Agnes with in-laws, Bill & Betty Tice and Don & Phyllis Boyd.
5. Agnes' family.

1. Agnes with granddaughter, Dara (Robertson) Marquis.
2. Dave & Agnes with great grandchildren: Ezekiel, Ezra, Clementine.
3. Agnes' daughter and son-in-law, Garry & Marcia Lauber.
4. Dave & Agnes' children and spouses.
5. Dave & Agnes.

1. Dave & Agnes piano duet.
2. Dave & Agnes' 50th wedding anniversary.
3. Agnes' best friend, Lois Greathouse.
4. Agnes modeling at age 89.
5. Dave & Agnes.

1. Agnes with sons, Dwight and David.
2. Agnes & Dave, Dreyson & Shiloh, Dwight & Dawn, Charlie & Dara.
3. Agnes' grandsons, Jeremiah and Landon Lauber.
4. Agnes' grandson, Landon Lauber, with his wife, Samantha, and their
   children: Ezekiel, Ezra, Clementine.

1. Agnes' grandson, Jeremiah, with his wife, Brandi, and their children:
   Leighton, Selah, Hadley.
2. Dave & Agnes with Marca & Garry Lauber, their son and daughter-in-law,
   Jeremiah & Brandi Lauber, and their children: Leighton, Selah, Hadley.
3. Agnes' daughter, Marcia.
4. Dave & Agnes.

FORGE RESOURCES AND OPPORTUNITIES

FORGE SPEAKERS & EVENTS
ForgeSpeakers.com

Needing someone to challenge your group to become passionate followers of Jesus who live with hearts on fire and lives on purpose? Book a Forge speaker for your next event!

FORGE EQUIPPING PROGRAMS for ALL AGES
ForgeForward.org/Equipping

Forge Equipping is not summer camp and training events "as usual." Forge challenges and equips people of all ages to become you-nique, lifelong Kingdom laborers in their everyday places.

FORGE BOOKS & RESOURCES
ForgeForward.org/Resources

Looking for a deeper relationship with God and practical ways to widen His Kingdom impact through your life? Forge has the resources you need.

THE FORGE APP
Essential Kingdom laboring tools right at your fingertips
TheForgeApp.org

JOIN THE MULTIPLYING MOVEMENT
Where everyday followers become Kingdom multipliers
MultiplyingMovements.com

FORGE VIDEO CONTENT
Subscribe to free video content at Youtube.com/ForgeForward

FORGE PODCAST
FuelForTheHarvest.com

FORGE DAILY TEXTS
Text SPARK to 33222 for one-sentence daily devotionals

NEEDING PRAYER?
Email us at Prayer@ForgeForward.org

CONTACT US
14485 E. Evans Avenue
Denver, Colorado 80014
303.745.8191
info@forgefoward.org

Learn more and get involved at ForgeForward.org